THE CHARGE OF THE LIGHT BRIGADE

Also from ALAN CAILLOU

CABOT CAIN Series
Assault on Kolchak
Assault on Loveless
Assault on Ming
Assault on Agathon
Assault on Fellawi
Assault on Aimata

TOBIN'S WAR Series
Dead Sea Submarine
Terror in Rio
Congo War Cry
Afghan Assault
Swamp War
Death Charge
The Garonsky Missile

MIKE BENASQUE Series
The Plotters
Marseilles
Who'll Buy My Evil
Diamonds Wild

IAN QUAYLE Series
A League of Hawks
The Sword of God

DEKKER'S DEMONS Series
Suicide Run
Blood Run

The Charge of the Light Brigade
A Journey to Orassia

Rogue's Gambit
Cairo Cabal
Bichu the Jaguar
The Walls of Jolo
The Hot Sun of Africa
The Cheetahs
Joshua's People
Mindanao Pearl
Khartoum
South from Khartoum
Rampage
The World is 6 Feet Square
The Prophetess
House on Curzon Street

THE CHARGE OF THE LIGHT BRIGADE

Copyright 2024 Eagle One Media, Inc.
Original Copyright 1968 Alan Caillou
All Rights Reserved.

No part of this book may be copied or retransmitted without the express written permission of the publisher and copyright holder. Limited use of excerpts may be used for journalistic or review purposes. Any similarities to individuals either living or dead is purely coincidental and unintentional except where fair use laws apply.

For further information visit the Caliber Comics website:
www.calibercomics.com

Cover Art by Armand Serrano

THE CRIMEAN WAR (1854-56) THEATER OF WAR

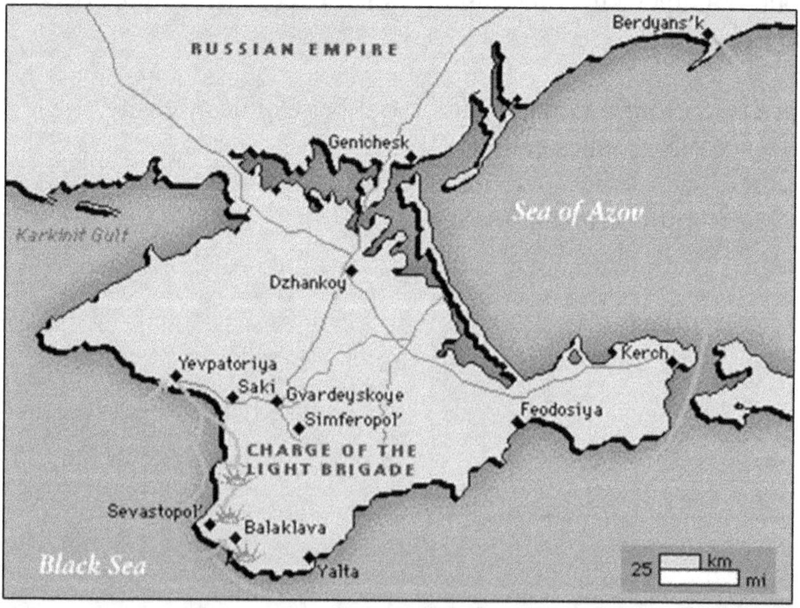

CHAPTER 1

They lay still and quiet in long lines across the lavender-scented grasses and listened to the sound of the Russian guns, three thousand of them in three thin red lines that stretched east and west along the bank of the river for more than a mile; and the guns were perilously close. Ahead of them, scorning to take cover in the grass, their officers patiently sat their horses, enduring the fire and offering themselves as targets because this was their duty and the privilege of their rank. Ahead of them, they could see the sun glinting on the Russian bayonets.

In their bright red and blue uniforms, with crossed white belts and shining, hard-peaked hats that caught the glare of the hot sun—those who were lucky enough not to be wearing their bearskins—with tight, choking collars to their jackets, and long muzzle-loading rifles, they lay in extended order and waited for the French to move into position.

By the first cold light of that morning in September; 1854, the British Grand Divisions which had come on the extended picnic that they all thought the assault on the Crimea would be had moved to face the great gray mass of the Russian armies. The River Alma was the first bastion on the drive toward Sebastopol, the fortified town that was to fall, so they hoped, within a few hours—or days at the most—to the combined British-French-Turkish assault. Though no one really counted the Turks for very much, they were just a ragged mob of undisciplined heathens. Not that the British counted much on the French, nor the French, for that matter, on the British; each of these armies was quite sure that in the last analysis the other would turn and run, as they always had run.

Fuir comme les Anglais, said the French, and the British reciprocated by calling it "taking French leave."

Marshal St. Arnaud himself had sketched out the plan for the battle, a plan which paid slight attention to the disposition of his own army and none at all to the disposition of the British. He had decided that the British would move off, on the left, at five-thirty in the morning to turn the Russians' flank. Indeed, when they did move, they were no more than three or four hours late. The French force, consisting of their First and Third Divisions, would then, while the Russian army's attention was thus hopefully distracted, make a frontal assault across the river, and the day would be won with glory to the Emperor Louis Napoleon, who fancied himself as masterly a strategist as his uncle had been. The lowly Turks would move with Bosquet's Division on the right, and the combined fleets of the Allies would move close inshore and give the enemy the pounding it so rightfully deserved. It was a simple, an overly simple plan, which the French Marshal had drawn up without bothering to consult his allies. Though, in theory, command was shared equally between the French and the British, the lowly Turks, who so far had borne the brunt of the fighting, and borne it well, had no part in the planning whatsoever.

But though the British were late, the French were later still, so that the Russians, faced with a British assault on their flank, turned to face them. Thus the belated French, scaling the steep banks of the cliff under which they had sheltered, now found themselves facing the enemy's flank; it was enough to make them stop and reconsider. And this is precisely what they did, and while they reconsidered, the British, already under fire from the enemy's guns, lay down in the grass and waited for someone to make up his mind what to do next. And, while they waited, many of them died.

St. Arnaud had not been selected by Louis Napoleon for his military competence, but rather because the Emperor wanted a commander who would unhesitatingly obey his own uninspired dictates in the field. And in his search for a commander who would not dispute his over-all authority and who could at the same time be relied upon to treat the English with the contempt they deserved, quite unhampered by the gentlemanly considerations that high military office entailed, he had been forced to send to Algeria, the testing ground of the French martial endeavor. His envoy, a certain Captain Fleury, had found an unscrupulous young lieutenant in the Foreign Legion, whose only claim to fame was that he had needlessly murdered five hundred Algerian rebels by sealing them in the cave where they had taken shelter. He had brought the young officer back to France (in spite of the fact that he had twice been driven out of the Army under a cloud) and had introduced him to the ambitious Emperor.

All that remained for St. Arnaud to do was to consolidate his position, and this he did with the timely slaughter of hundreds of peaceful Parisians who might have objected to Louis Napoleon's overthrow of the Republic and seizure of the throne.

It was all very simple and in character, and soon the onetime lieutenant of the Foreign Legion, untrained in battle, was commanding the field armies of Europe's mightiest power.

So now, while St. Arnaud was making up his mind, the British waited. Their commander was Lord Raglan, an amiable and kindly man who had lost an arm with the Duke of Wellington and whose answer to every question was another question: What would the Duke have done? This was the question he was asking himself now, and the answer he found was quite straightforward. Under these circumstances, no doubt, the Duke would have attacked.

The men lay in the hot sun while the cannonballs of the Russian gunners scattered themselves with deadly effect among their lines, and Raglan summoned his aide, one Captain Nolan (who was soon to engrave his name on the matrix of history) and gave him the requisite order, though giving orders was very much against his gentle nature; he much preferred to suggest. "Go quietly," he said. "Don't gallop." After all, it would be unpardonable for undue haste to suggest to the enemy, who stood in massed columns such a little way off, that the hesitancy of the French could cause any alarm, or even impatience, in the stolid British breast.

And so, the three thin lines rose up out of the ground. For an hour and a half the lines had lain there, while the wounded stoically endured their fate. Brigadier General Sir Colin Campbell commanding the Highland Brigade had ridden his horse up and down the lines of mutilated, waiting men, telling them quietly, "Whoever is wounded must lie where he is till a bandsman comes to attend him..." It was the fashion then for wounded not to be attended to until the last shot of the battle had been fired, and all they could do was wait in their agony for that happy moment.

The cannonballs rolled at them, bouncing along the springy turf, some of them burning long scores of brown in the green because they had been heated red-hot in the gunners' fire. Also the scattered musket fire, not so effective at this range, was none the less taking its toll.

The lines re-formed, dressing by the right as if they had been on a parade ground, extending once more in correct alignment of immaculately-formed divisions. It was the most disciplined army that history had ever known, and history would never again know this kind of blind, robot-like obedience to order. Their straps were white with pipe clay, their buttons still shining brightly; and shoulder to shoulder, with their officers riding ahead of them, they marched proudly into the waiting Russian guns, not breaking the line—it was not considered correct behavior even to sidestep an oncoming cannonball—nor losing a parade ground step. They strode down the gentle slope and into the river, and they kept their line of dressing; some of them fell into deep water and drowned and others were swept away by the force of the water, but still they kept their line. They held their rifles and their ammunition pouches over their heads to keep them dry, and when they reached the bank and struggled through the mud and onto the grass again they paused while the officers once more dressed the lines into precise formation—many of them falling now, but the remainder attending to their drill—then moved on steadily while wounded or dead men fell to cannonballs, grapeshot, musket fire, and canisters.

All, that is, except the brigade on the right. Here, the configuration of the riverbank had done something even the Russian guns had been unable to do—it had thrown the British line into disorder. A bend in the river and a sudden narrowing of a deep inlet had forced the brigade on the right flank here into a narrow defile, a funnel of men pouring up out of the water in chaos, and they were directly under a battery of Russian guns on their own flank—guns that should, by now, have been too busy with the French to have caused the brigade much alarm, if only the French had been there. The troops were swarming ashore in a crowd, disordered, disoriented, and confused, and at their head rode a man who wasn't even supposed to be there—Brigadier General Codrington.

Codrington had not been posted to the Crimea at all. He had considered this an intolerable affront—after all, Britain had not fought a war for forty years, and it was time for an honest soldier to be in battle again. So he had made his own way out to the battleground by boat and rail and horse, and the amiable Lord

Raglan had promptly given him a command. He had never seen active service before, and when he saw his men crowded into a solid amorphous mass that was dangerously out of kilter with all the parade ground tactics he had learned; he did what any other man of staunch courage would do. He pointed his sword at the enemy and yelled, "Attack!"

The point at which he had chosen to throw his men happened to be the center of the Russian forces, the redoubt on which they were anchored, and without a doubt the strongest point of their line. It was a battery of fourteen heavy guns, protected by a massive earthwork, which had become known as the "Great Redoubt."

On his white Arabian pony, Codrington swarmed up the steep bank and rode hell-for-leather for the guns, and his men broke into a cheer and followed him. The Russians poured out of their defenses to meet them, and head-on the two forces collided, the Russians in their long gray coats, and the British in their ceremonial blue and red. They fired their guns at close range, and they used their bayonets to good effect, and the two thousand men of the Light Brigade found themselves close-pressed and surrounded by ten thousand men of Menshikov's ill-disciplined but dangerous army. They fought till the Russians broke and ran and they entrenched themselves behind the parapets of the redoubt, and they waited for the inevitable counterattack.

It came, soon enough. Four battalions of the Vladimir Regiment, led by Prince Gortchakoff and General Kvetzinski, each of whom subsequently was to claim that *he* led their attack and that the other wasn't even there, came pouring out of the folds in the ground to retake the defenses.

But in the British lines someone—and history does not record who it was—mistook the enemy Russians for the friendly French and that someone yelled the order: "Hold your fire, it's the French!" And the fire was held as the Russians advanced; the French had not yet even crossed the river.

THE CHARGE OF THE LIGHT BRIGADE

But now, one of those strange things happened upon which great battles turn. Faced with the sudden and quite inexplicable cessation of fire, the Russians halted their advance. And while they halted, another Russian column appeared and took up the challenge, and someone in the British ranks ordered the retreat to be sounded. It is not known who gave the order, and it was promptly countermanded. But the time had come for discussion, since here was an untenable position that ought, in theory, to be abandoned. Yet, can a force of strong men so easily be expected to retreat under the eyes of the watching and cowardly French across the river, waiting no doubt for the battle to be won before they should continue their advance?

And so, it was time for a conference. The junior officers gathered together to decide what to do; and in the fashion of the time, they stood together atop the parapets to argue in order to inspire confidence in their men and to assert their own bravery—which no one would doubt anyway—under the withering fire of the Russians. The first Russian column had taken up its advance again, and now both enemy columns, firing as they came, were moving in to attack the stronghold.

And all the officers standing there were shot down.

Now there was no one left in authority, and, after all, the retreat had indeed been sounded. The men began to fall back on the river.

But now, down below on the river bank, the rest of the British army was emerging from the mud: the Highlanders, the Coldstreams, the Scot Fusiliers, and the Grenadiers, in bearskins, Highland bonnets, tartans, and red pantaloons, and they were moving up the hill always dressed in immaculate formation—to the rescue. The men from the redoubt, who had been ordered to retreat and were prudently doing so, broke through the oncoming infantry lines in the flight to the river, but the lines were redressed until they were once more in parade ground order. And now, eight separate Russian columns were moving down the hill from Kouranie to meet them, eight columns at the gallop, brandishing swords and firing muskets; but now the infantry was ready.

The Duke of Cambridge gave the order: "The Line will advance, firing."

They advanced, and they fired. The Russian columns broke and ran, and the battle of the Alma was over and won.

And nothing had been gained. There were two thousand British casualties on the battlefield. One-third of the entire force lay dead. The French, who had not been entirely successful in avoiding scattered skirmishes with the enemy, suffered sixty men killed.

The wounded were dying. There was almost no medical service in this army, and whatever medical supplies the army had carried when it had left England had been left behind at the staging area at Varna, in Bulgaria, as too cumbersome to carry, even though in Varna itself a dreadful cholera epidemic had killed eight hundred British soldiers and ten thousand French. There was almost no water. When they had left the Old Fort for Sebastopol—a ten day march—they had carried food for three days and water for one. Now, though the river was close by, most of it had been turned into a muddy quagmire by the trampling feat of two armies. There was no transportation for the wounded; there were no carts or even stretchers. Those lucky enough to be attended to were carried by their fellows down to the river, across its mud, and five miles along the road to the little town of Balaklava, population less than a hundred, where a British ship had put into the harbor to remove the wounded.

As for the rest, those who were not so fortunate, they lay there in the cool of the evening, and they waited for death to overtake them.

One of them was a young man named Alexander Wilfred Kirkaldy. He was twenty-one years old, and a cannonball had broken his right leg in two places. A musket ball had torn a small

THE CHARGE OF THE LIGHT BRIGADE

piece of flesh from his left shoulder, and he was bleeding badly. He lay there through the evening till the sky was dark, and when the moon came up he rolled over on his stomach and prayed for death to take away the pain.

CHAPTER 2

He awoke to feel rough hands pulling at his shoulders, and he was being dragged along the ground toward the water.

His first thought was that the bandsmen had come at last, that they'd overlooked him the first time when they carelessly checked the battlefield, all five square miles of it. He figured they had come back in the darkness to see if any others were left there who could be helped.

And then, as consciousness began to come back to him, he heard voices speaking quietly in a language he did not understand, and there was a sudden onrush of alarm. He would have cried out, except that the pain flooding over his body had caused him to bite his tongue neatly through, and his mouth was swollen and bloody. He opened his eyes, and there was a bearded face peering into his, and he heard the strange language again, and then someone said in English:

"Don't worry, boy, you're in good hands." It was the rough, coarse accent of the English from the South. And then an old man was bending over him, an old man in rags with a week-old stubble of white beard, and the voice said again, "What's your name, boy?"

He forced the blood away from his mouth, swallowing

hard. He said, "My name's Kirk—Alexander Kirkaldy. They call me Kirk..."

The old man nodded "Aye, a one of the Highlanders, no doubt?"

"No. The Lancers. Seventeenth...Lancers." It was hard to talk.

He saw the old man frown. "A cavalryman?" He felt the groping hand in the darkness go to the epaulettes, as though seeking confirmation. "Aye, a cavalryman. But then, what are you doing on this field, boy? This was an infantry battle, the Lancers were across on the other side of the river."

Kirk could hardly breathe. "Dispatch...dispatch riding, My horse was shot from under me, and...they put me in the line with the infantry."

The old man laughed. "It's no place for a horseman now, is it? Why didn't you make your way back to your own unit?"

Kirk said wearily, "Is it the time to argue, old man? Just tell me...tell me who you are."

He could see others in the group now, moving like dark ghosts in the night, in silence. They were all around him, six or eight of them, picking up fallen muskets, rifling through dead bodies. He saw a dead trooper being stripped of his boots, and he said, "For shame, stealing from the dead..."

The old mem grinned, "Not stealing, boy, getting ourselves some ammunition, some good muskets. The fight's not over yet." He added, "And my name's Jack. Jack Bates, late of Her Majesty's glorious Navy, but now a deserter, boy, and fighting this bloody war the way it's supposed to be fought. Who put that rag around your leg?"

"I did."

"You put it on too tight, boy. But it doesn't matter, the foot's near gone anyway, you'll no doubt lose it in a day or two." Strong hands were plucking away the rags he'd wound tightly there to try and stop the blood pouring out, and the pain all came back now that the leg was losing its numbness.

Kirk said, worrying about it, "A deserter? All of you?"

"No, just me." The old man grinned. "You heard of the Bashi-Bazouk?"

"Yes, I've heard of them."

The word sent a tremor of excitement through him, a tingling at the back of his neck. The Bashi-Bazouk were the Turkish irregulars, every man of them a professional bandit. They had ridden in from the mountains when Sultan Mahmoud had announced to his people that he'd declared war on Turkey's traditional enemy, the Russians. (Though the truth of the matter was that Russia had taken the first steps to war, leaving the actual declaration to the Turks for the sake of what they hoped would be worldwide approbation, a Christian country defending itself against the terrors threatened by the heathen; it hadn't worked out that way at all, as nothing in this foolish war was ever to work out properly.)

The Bashi-Bazouk had ridden hard from all over Asia Minor on their fast little ponies, armed to the teeth with an assortment of stolen or hereditary weapons, terrorizing the populations they passed through, demanding—and getting; no one would argue with them—all the supplies they needed for a holy war. Some of them had come from as far afield as Kurdistan, riding hard across the mountains and over the plains, in disordered, menacing groups of ten, fifty, a hundred. The Russians were terrified of them; and so, to tell the truth, were the English and the French because, although they fought well enough when the right enemy was pointed out to them (when they were aimed, so to speak, in the right direction by the officers of the Nizam, the Turkish regular army), they would also turn on anything in sight when there wasn't enough military endeavor around to satisfy their warlike ambitions.

They were brave men without mercy; and they were deadly.

THE CHARGE OF THE LIGHT BRIGADE

So now Kirk trembled. He said, hesitantly, "Are you their prisoner?"

The old man laughed. "God bless you, boy, I'm one of them! Jack Bates, once master gunner on Her Majesty's Frigate *Arethusa* as fine a ship as a man could lay eyes on, fifty guns... And all sail, boy, none of them newfangled paddles or screws to fool around with, just an honest fighting ship. You heard what we done at Odessa?"

The pain was seeping over Kirk in waves, and he shook his head from side to side, a boy fighting away a boy's tears. Jack Bates was straightening out the leg, and another man came up and helped; and someone put his foot in the boy's crotch and pulled on the ankle, and Kirk screamed, and Bates said calmly, "They fired on us under a flag of truce, did you know that? You can't never trust them Russians." (He did not know that the truce had never been arranged, that the Russians quite naturally had fired on a small enemy boat that had come blandly into the harbor to take off the British Consul if, by chance, he wanted to leave before hostilities actually started.)

He said, grumbling: "They fired on our flag of truce, boy, that's the kind of enemy we're up agin. So they told us, the brass, to teach them a lesson, and we went in and taught them. There was a fort on the hill above the town, and we sailed in under her guns and fired a broadside, the port side first, then the bow guns as we tacked, the starboard next, and then the stern as we came about, four broadsides, boy, one after the other just like it used to be in the old days. Three times we sailed in, and three times we used our guns, and when we'd finished there wasn't nothing left of that battery but a mess of smoking ruins. Does that hurt, boy? A little bit?"

They were twisting the bones into place; you could hear them grating against each other. Bates went on as he worked, talking fast and carefully to take the patient's mind off the pain:

"They cheered us when we took up our position with the

Fleet again. Coming across the water you could hear the cheers for the good old *Arethusa*. Never was a fighting ship like her; boy. Oh, they hit us once or twice, they said that fort was impregnable, and it nearly was, but not to the *Arethusa*. But all the damage they done was one small boat shot clean off our decks, the captain's gig, so it didn't matter too much, wouldn't you say?"

Kirk did not reply, and Bates peered down into his face and said to no one in particular; "Lord stone the crows, the boy's fainted! That's the Army for you, he's fainted! In the Navy, we'd throw him overboard for that. Here, help him up onto my shoulder."

None of the others could properly understand him. But they'd been together, this oddly assorted group, for three weeks now, and signs were enough, with a few words of French, or Arabic, or Turkish, or anything else thrown in. So they hoisted the limp form over the old man's shoulders, and he stood up straight and strong in spite of his sixty-odd years. He made a gesture with his head to the others, and they followed. Because, although they couldn't always understand what he was trying to say to them, somehow they had come to accept the fact that this was the best fighting man among them, and as such he had become one of them.

They followed him down to the river and there Jean-Marie Pierre de la Tour Epernon was waiting for them, gathering rifles and cartridges and stacking them in orderly piles by the water's edge. He looked up as he saw them coming down the slope toward him, and he said languidly, "We do not want bodies, *mon vieux*, we want arms."

He gestured toward the piles he had set up, and said, "Eighteen muskets, four hundred cartridges, and all the cannonballs we can ever use. But how to move them? We need carts..."

He was a small, slight, wiry man in his early thirties, a

soldier from General Bosquet's Division. A few days before, in the long march across the Crimean plain, he had gotten into an argument with three of the Zouaves who had come from Varna, thirty thousand of them, to bolster the French forces. A trifling argument over the disposal of a captured Russian saber, but Epernon was not the kind of man to listen to heathen arguments when simpler courses were open to him. He had taken the saber that was the object of such acrimonious contention and had run two of the Zouaves through with it, killing both in one swift second of fury. And he had been on the run ever since.

He was a man of easy manner whose only desire had always been to heap glory on himself in the name of an Emperor for whom he had nothing but contempt. But he was a brave man, a good soldier; and now he was searching that glory for himself by continuing the war in his own personal style; alone, or with the help of others he might meet on the roadside. The roadsides were full of stragglers; some of them were deserters, some were wounded who were trying to find their way back to the base, and some were simply lost. And among them there were always good men to be found, men like Jack Bates, *le salaud Anglais*, who was a decent fellow in spite of the accident of his birth.

They laid Kirk down on the sweet-smelling grass, its lavender scent more pronounced in the dew of the dark night, and they lit a fire and brewed coffee. The Turks cut lumps of goat meat with their long knives and threw them into the flames, not waiting for the logs to burn down into embers, while they smoked their clay or calabash pipes and sat there stolid and silent, with the firelight playing on their weather-beaten faces, listening to the strange mixture of tongues the infidels spoke among themselves. One of them, whose name was Mahmoud Enzir, spoke English as he had worked once as a servant in the Consulate at Constantinople—until the police had arrested him for stealing the Consul's silver dinner service and trying to sell it to the Germans at their Embassy.

He smoked a long briar pipe he had found in a dead soldier's pocket and he poked it at Kirk and asked, grunting, "If he lives, will he fight?"

Jack Bates shrugged. "That's all you think of, Mahmoud, can he fight? I'm thinking a young boy like that shouldn't be left to die on the battlefield. Sure he'll fight, he's a British fighting man, better'n any of you heathens any day, even if the good Lord never did bless him with the chance to join the Queen's Navy. He'll fight, you'll see."

Epernon said drily, "Like all the others, he will want to be taken back to his base, so that once more he can step out bravely at the command of his foolish officers."

"You speak for your own officers, Frenchy." Bates' voice held no rancor; and Epernon laughed. He said:

"To each of us, the other is worse. But to each of us also, his own officers are the best. You realize what that means, my friend? It means that you and I both have been so conditioned that we accept without question the superiority of those in command who have spent all their lives teaching us to respect that superiority. It is very sad, is it not, that we cannot think for ourselves and decide for ourselves just whom we should respect?"

Bates said calmly "In the Queen's Navy, we call it discipline. Did your watch your fellows advance yesterday morning?"

Epernon's face clouded, "I watched them. I was in Bourlouk village, stealing some wine, when they burned it. I watched them leave their pretty little camp, I watched them go a few hundred yards, and I watched them stop and wait for someone else to do the fighting."

Bates said drily, "They stopped to make their coffee." And Epernon grinned delightedly and said, "But of course, a man cannot fight, if perhaps a fight is forced upon him; unless there is coffee in his stomach. And you will admit, the British were late, as always, so it was necessary for the French to wait for them to catch up."

"Did they have to wait quite so long? Till the bloody battle was over?"

But Epernon would not rise to the gibe. He laughed again, showing his white teeth. He had shaved that day, and his face was smooth and shining in the firelight: "The Turks told me that General Menshikov rode off with seven battalions of infantry to outflank your people's attack, but turned back when he came under the fire of the ships lying off the coast. The *French* ships, *mon vieux*."

Bates said, "You know, Frenchy, I don't care what side they're on, just so they're in the right arm of the service. And, like I always say, it's the Navy every time. British or French or Russian or even Turkish, for all I know. You can always trust the Navy."

The meat in the flames was burning, and the ripe smell of it was on the air. One of the Turks leaned in and pulled out a hunk with his bare hands, and he went over to Kirk where he lay by the water and crouched down on his heels to look at him, tearing the meat and munching it. He stared for a while, and then he spoke to Mahmoud, and Mahmoud said, "If the boy does not eat, he will die. He has lost much blood."

Bates scratched his head with a strong, calloused hand. "Soon as he comes round, we'll give him food."

Mahmoud got to his feet. He cut strips of fat from the meat and put them in a tin can and wedged the can in among the flames. "In my county," he said, "the best thing. We give him fat to drink, we make a man of him."

They heard Kirk groan, and Bates went across and sat on the grass beside him, his long legs splayed out and his body arched forward. He said gently, "The pain'll be with you for a long time, boy, you better get used to it. That leg's good and busted."

They had strapped two sticks to his shattered leg and bound a tourniquet around the thigh.

Kirk mumbled and tried to speak, and he said at last, shuddering, "Not my leg...my shoulder."

Bates leaned in and plucked at the soiled blue cloth, and his probing fingers found a hole there, and he pulled away the stuff and looked and said, "Oh, for Christ's sake!..."

He pulled out his knife and tested the sharpness of the blade on his thumbnail and got up and walked back to the others. He said: "Who's got a good sharp knife? Mine wouldn't cut melted butter, got to put an edge on it one of these days."

Mahmoud pulled out his long curved dagger, grinned, and said, "You want to shave, Ingles?"

"The boy's got a musket ball in his shoulder; it'll have to come out."

Epernon was already getting to his feet. He said, "Give me the sharp knife, Jacques, you hold him down."

The Turks went on chewing their meat, and Bates held the boy's arms firmly on the grass, and Epernon probed with his fingers till Kirk began to scream, and he looked at Bates and Bates raised up the boy's head and hit him, just once, hard, on the base of the jaw. When the head went shack, he said, "All right, Frenchy, now, quick as you can."

Epernon said calmly, "A moment, no more." He dug the knife in deep and levered out the ball, and then he looked at the edge and said, wonderingly, "How do they make a crude knife like this so sharp, I wonder? Really, I must find out how they do it."

Mahmoud was moving toward them, his two hands held together and filled with wood ash. Without a word, he squatted down and began to pack the ash into the wound, and he crouched there, watching, while Epernon found a piece of rag and wrapped it right around the wound, grumbling because the rag was not long enough to reach the back of the shoulder blade for a strong knot.

Mahmoud said roughly, "It is nothing, a bullet wound." He began to laugh and said, "He make plenty noise, a woman."

"The boy's hurt, you bloody heathen," Bates said affably. "He's hurt bad, and if we don't take good care of him, he's going to die."

Mahmoud showed his strong white teeth in the firelight, thumped hard at his own stomach, and said: "Here, in the belly, that's where you get hurt, you die. In the shoulder, in the arm, the leg, it don't make no trouble. Allah gave man two arms, two legs, so he lose one in battle it don't make no harm. But he only give one belly, you lose that, you got trouble."

He went over to the fire and brought back the tin of scalding fat. He began to blow on it, and then he handed it to Epernon and said, "Here, you give this woman fat, she get well again, don't scream no more."

Epernon said, "You're a savage, Mahmoud, an uncultured savage." And Mahmoud threw back his head and roared with laughter.

When the fat had cooled off a little, they held Kirk's head and poured some of it between his blue lips, dark-blue against the white pain-racked face with the pimples that the food and the water had caused. Kirk splattered and came round and said vaguely, one hand groping, "Dad? Dad? Is that you, Dad?"

Bates said, "You're going to be all right, boy. If a man can talk in the state you're in, he's going to be all right." He brushed the lank hair, dust-grimed and unwashed, away from the white forehead and said, "You know what, Kirk? I'm going to find you a cart to ride in. You ride with us for a few days...you'll soon be well again."

Epernon said sourly, "A cart! If we find a cart, I want it for those muskets."

High on the Kourganie Hills, to the south and the east of the river, 212 of the Bashi-Bazouk were reforming. They had blundered into the solid defenses of the Little Redoubt, half a mile to the east of the place where Codrington's men had so distinguished themselves, if only in chaos; and there, the Russian cavalry, more than two thousand of them, had made a sudden sortie into their midst and cut them to pieces. Many of the Bashi-Bazouk had lost their weapons, the guns they had brought in their long ride south; and to these bandits, a gun was the right arm. But the battlefield was thick with good British and French muskets, and this little group was gathering them together to resupply their main force, or to bury in haylofts and vineyards where they could be found quickly the next time.

But Bates said firmly, "All right, Frenchy, two carts. One for the guns and one for the boy."

"And where will you find two carts, may I ask? The British have requisitioned every vehicle for a hundred miles around to carry their officers' wives and the other little luxuries without which they cannot endure this...this pique-nique of theirs."

"In Bourlouk village, maybe."

"I told you, I was in Bourlouk, there is nothing there. I was there when the Allies burned it."

Bates said sourly, "When the French burned it, and can you tell me why they had to do that?"

Epernon shrugged. "There was always the chance there would be some Russians there. After all, they had not destroyed the bridge that crosses the river there, so perhaps the assumption was a natural one."

Bates said, "And by the looks of it, that Russky general, what's his name?..."

"Menshikov."

"Menshikov didn't even know there was two fords across the river he was trying to defend, so maybe he didn't even know the bridge was there either. Thank God their officers are no better than ours."

Epernon said firmly, "But there will be no carts there. No carts, no supplies, no nothing."

"All right. Down the river a ways there's another village, what's its name?"

"Alma Tamack. And no carts there either."

"Stone the crows, Frenchy, you don't hold out much hope to a man, do you?" Bates got to his fest. He said: "I'll take Mahmoud and two of the men with me. Two carts, it will need four men to handle them up the hill."

Epernon shrugged. "You waste your time, my friend, but time is all we have, is it not? It need not be too carefully hushanded. And it is a good night for a stroll along the bank of the river, with nothing but meditation for a pastime." He added dreamily, "In my home, there is a river, too, a fine river that wanders through my father's estate, a slow, shallow river with yellow flowers and silver fish. It is a long way from this sad country... All right, get your carts, we will wait for you here."

On the other side of the ridge; across the wide plain that led to the River Tchernaya, the exhausted armies of the Allies, shivering in the cold, were sleeping round the campfires that nightly indicated their positions to the spies of the Russian General Menshikov. (Unlike the gentlemanly British and French, the Russians had no inhibitions about spying out the enemy's dispositions before an attack.)

But here, close by the quagmire that once had been a broad river, that was now churned up into a muddy swamp, the little group feasted on their goat's milk, and gorged themselves on the figs they had taken from the gardens, and drank the wine they had looted from the little white-painted houses with their mud walls and thatched roofs.

They were dressed in rags, and they carried swords, and knives, and long curved daggers, and some of them had muskets and lances and bayonets. Their faces were dark and like deep-grained leather, and their eyes were black and alert and constantly moving. Here, many miles from their homes, they were at war with the whole world, for the whole world had always been their enemy.

And they listened to the groans of the boy who was called Kirk as he twisted and turned in a pain-filled sleep. Once or twice they turned to look at him, and grunted their contempt for the sounds of the pain.

CHAPTER 3

Bourlouk had been burned to the ground, and there was nothing left but charred mounds of hard-caked mud and a few still smoldering timbers.

But the nearby village called Alma Tamack was still standing, though deserted. A small riverside cluster of thirty or forty mud huts; with two dirt roads bisecting it in the middle. The rubble wall around the central well had caved in, and there were bullet holes scarring the whitewashed walls; a stray cannonball had crashed through the heavy wooden door of the tiny church.

They walked through the streets, if they could be called streets, in silence, their sandaled feet making no sound at all. And Mahmoud whispered a warning and drew back into the shadows. Bates froze, then slipped into the darkness also, away from the white reflections of the moon. Mahmoud pointed, and said, his voice very low: "A woman."

Bates looked at him and shrugged, and Mahmoud said, insisting, "One of *your* women." Bates frowned; an English woman, here? It did not seem possible.

And then he saw her, quite clearly. She was moving out of the shadows of the stables that were ahead of them, crossing the dirt road and entering one of the houses, and she carried an unlit kerosene lamp in her hand, a small slimy and light-footed figure, moving with caution but with an air of determination as well as though the dangers here in this deserted village had to be faced, come what may. She was not hiding, but she was also not showing herself more than was necessary, moving quickly and lithely in the shadows.

Bates looked at Mahmoud and said, "She can't be alone, you know that?"

Mahmoud nodded. "Better we see who she is. Better we see who else is here, maybe trouble."

Bates was conscious that the potential trouble was only on his own account. There might be stray British or French troops here, or even a strong armed force out raiding, and the sudden presence among them of an Englishman dressed in castoff Turkish rags... The Bashi-Bazouk, fighting against a common enemy, were known as Allies, wild and savage though they were. But a deserter among them would have short shrift from his own men. He said, "I'll come with you."

Mahmoud signaled to the others to wait, and watched while the two of them took up careful positions, one on either side of the house the woman had entered. Their guns were cocked as this was part of the pattern of their lives, with every shadow hostile to them.

Bates and Mahmoud moved slowly, carefully, up to the thick walls of the house, and stood close by the open hole in the wall that was its window; there was scarcely any sound inside. There was just the scrape of a match being drawn through its fold of paper and then the strong, offensive odor of its poisonous gases. Then there was the light, flaring brightly to the splutter of sparks, and then, at last, the steady yellow glow of a burning wick.

Inside the house someone said; "Can you hear me, Lieutenant? Can you hear me?" It was a woman's voice, a young girl's voice, and there was no answer. In a moment, the voice came again, anguished now: "Oh God, dear God..." There was the sound of gentle sobbing.

Bates touched Mahmoud's shoulder and jerked his head in a motion that meant: Come with me. Together they moved toward the door, half-open on its unstable leather hinges. Their rifles were loaded and ready. In the clear light of the lamp, they saw the young woman, her back toward them, her head buried in her hands as she sobbed. And on the low string-bed in front of her, an officer in the uniform of the Inniskillings was stretched out, his face white, his eyes and his mouth wide open in death. There was no one else in the room.

Bates said, hesitantly, "Ma'am...?"

The young woman spun round with a gasp. There was terror in her eyes when she saw the rags the two men were wearing, when she saw their beard-stubbled, unkempt faces. The Turks were good fighters in spite of the contempt the other Allies had for them, the best fighters, if the truth were known, they'd ever had the good fortune to fight with. But, and especially, for a woman alone at night, the stories of their lusts were legend.

Bates said quickly, "It's all right Ma'am, I'm an Englishman, a sailor off the *Arethusa*, and him..." he jerked a grimy thumb, "Oh, he's a Turk all right, but he won't harm you Ma'am, not while I'm around."

Her voice was low and hollow-sounding. "An Englishman? A sailor?" She could not believe it.

Bates said cheerfully, "Yes Ma'am, that's what I used to be." As though afraid she would doubt his word, he pulled open the coarse homespun shirt he wore, the seams torn off at the shoulders to leave his muscular arms bare, and showed her with pride the tattoo marks on his chest. He said proudly, "You see, Ma'am?"

It was a stylized portrait of Queen Victoria, in red and blue and green, with a wreath of roses round her neck and the legend underneath, in a flowery, elaborate hand: *For Mother and the Queen.* He grinned and said, "You see, Ma'am? Had that done fifteen years ago, the day the good Queen got married to that young Albert." He said again, "You see? An Englishman, in spite of these Turkish rags. So, don't be afraid, Ma'am, you got nothing to fear."

The woman did not answer. She was trembling.

Mahmoud said, grinning, "Me too, lady, good man. No trouble this time."

She turned away and looked down at the dead lieutenant. She said, very quietly, "He's gone. He was alive, and I hoped that I could... I went to find a lamp, and when I got back he was dead."

Bates said sympathetically, "Your husband, Ma'am?"

Many of the British officers had brought their wives with them out from England; some of them had even brought their whole families. After all, this incursion among the Russians was merely a parade ground exercise; it was—or at least it had started out as—a picnic they could all enjoy in the warm Crimean sun.

She shook her head. "No. I don't know who he is. An officer of the Inniskillings, by his uniform."

"And you, Ma'am?" It seemed a discourtesy to ask a lady what she might be doing here in this grubby little village in the middle of the night.

She said, "I'm a nurse, sailor. What's your name?"

"Bates, Ma'am. Jack Bates, HMS *Arethusa*. But not anymore. Now I'm fighting with the Bashi-Bazouk."

"You mean... on loan from the Navy?" It didn't seem to make sense.

"No Ma'am. A deserter." There was no use hiding it.

She held her head very high. "That's not a very good word, sailor."

Bates said equably, "No Ma'am, but I've got my reasons." He was gaining courage from her implied disapproval. "And I've got my work to do, only... Well, I can't hardly leave you alone in a Russian village in the middle of the night, even though there ain't...isn't no one else here. You tell me where you belong, Ma'am, I'll take time out to see that you get there safely. It's the least an Englishman can do."

She sat down heavily on the three-legged wooden stool that stood on the dirt foot, pounded hard and well swept. "No, thank you...I came here alone, I can get back alone."

Bates was frowning, remembering something she had said. "A nurse, you said? I never knew we had nurses out here, Ma'am. All I seen is a few old pensioners helping out."

The nursing service had not yet been established. It was the fashion to detail any soldier who was not competent for the serious matter of fighting—the habitual drunks, the cowards, the lame—to look after the wounded. These were the "bandsmen," and they were reinforced by a few elderly pensioners who had come out from England to stay with the army they loved and to revel in the glory that was soon to cover it again after so much peace. But most of them had been killed off in the terrible cholera epidemic that had swept through the army as it marched across Bulgaria on its way to the Crimea.

Remembering it now, Bates said, "I was in that epidemic, and we could have done with a few lady nurses ourselves."

She looked up at him. "The cholera?"

"Yes, Ma'am. It's a germ they say, like a little insect, that gets carried on the wind. The wind's damp in Bulgaria, and that made it worse. We took the ships out to sea to get away from it, but it didn't seem to do no good. They say that the wind followed us out to sea and brought the germs along with it, that we 'a' been better off to lie in the harbor, but... I don't know. We lost eighty men on the *Arethusa*, three hundred on the Britannia."

Staring at the dead officer's white face, she said, "No, it's not like that at all. It's nothing to do with the wind. I work in a hospital in Plymouth, sailor, and I can tell you..." She broke off, knowing that it would do no good.

But Bates was puzzled. He said, "You're a long way from Plymouth here, Ma'am, and if it's not impolite to ask... I'd give a deal to know what you're doing in Alma Tamack in the middle of the night, all alone and all. It doesn't seem to make much sense to a man like me, with no education to teach him the use of reason."

She looked up at him, staring at him, trying to fathom the workings of his mind. She said at last, very slowly, "There are many, very many men left to die on the battlefields, because there's no one to care for them who knows anything at all about...about medicine, or nursing..." Her face was white with exhaustion, her eyes dark-rimmed. "And so, I asked them for help, and they gave me a man and a cart, and I spend my days searching the fields for those who have been left behind to die. Sometimes they crawl to shelter, and the bandsmen miss them, or sometimes the bandsmen are too drunk to know what they're doing, and so..." She brushed a lock of long hair from her face and said fiercely, "*Someone* has to take care of these men! So all day, and all night too, sometimes, I take my little cart and my bodyguard, and I search." She looked across at the still form of the young lieutenant. "He would have been the tenth in the last two days. And I was too late to save him."

Bates said, recovering his good humor, "Well, if we got nurses now... Been stories going around for a long time that they was going to send us some."

"No, not yet, I came here with my father. He's Mr. Enderly."

It seemed as though the name were sufficient introduction. Bates screwed up his eyes and echoed, "Mr. Enderly?"

"One of the merchants."

The British Navy, going off to invade Russian territory, had obligingly given a lift to a group of merchants who had business to conduct with the Russians and had landed them at

THE CHARGE OF THE LIGHT BRIGADE

Odessa.

She said, "My father will be coming back to the Fleet soon, and we'll go home, but while I'm here...there's so much sickness here, and no one doing anything about it." Her voice was angry now. "They drink water out of stinking, fetid pools and then they blame the damp wind for epidemics! They wait till the pork is rotting before they issue it, and then they wonder why men take dysentery and drop like flies! And they leave the wounded to die, like...like this man!" She turned back to the dead lieutenant and said, "You know why he died? A scratch on the thigh, a piece of metal from a canister, perhaps, and he bled to death because there was no one nearby who knew what to do."

Bates said stolidly, "It's not that, Ma'am, if you'll excuse me. You can't be expected to stop in the middle of a fight to take care of a man who's been hit. Where would the army be if they was all looking after the wounded all the time? That's a job for the bandsmen, after the fighting is done."

She said shortly, "Well, it's not right. I don't care how much you accept, the incompetence, the stupidity..." She was aware of a certain look in Bates eyes and she broke off and said more gently, "Is that why you deserted, Bates?"

Grudgingly: "Yes, Ma'am, more or less. Forty years in the Navy, give or take a week or two, and when I saw the games they was playing... They're not *trying* to this war, Ma'am, that's the trouble. They came out here ten thousand miles from home on a bloody picnic, begging your pardon, Ma'am, a picnic. No planning, no knowledge of what they want to get done, and for some of us... Well, for some of us who fought the French in the old days, this is not the way a war is won. But me and my friends, we're doing our bit in our own way, more than I ever done on board the *Arethusa*, good ship though she was. We're doing our bit, and that's all that matters. Forty years I threw away to do what I know is right, and that wasn't easy." He said, with simple pride. "But I'm glad I done it."

"And now, Bates?"

"Now, Ma'am, now I'm looking for a cart, to carry one of our men, he's wounded."

"A Bashi-Bazouk? The Turks don't carry their wounded." She said brutally, "They shoot them."

"Not this man, they won't shoot him. He's one of us. An English soldier, just a boy. A leg smashed by a cannonball, and a musketball in the shoulder. Lying out in the field there since the battle yesterday afternoon, and lucky if he lives to tell about it."

She said sharply, "And what have you done about it?"

He shrugged. "Well, we bound him np good and tight, and we put wood ash on his wounds, and we've got him laid out comfortably by the river and... Well, now we wait."

"You wait for him to die or live, just like all the others."

"Well, of course. What else is there we can do, Ma'am?"

She got to her feet, a thin, tired, and exhausted woman, driven by her own anger. She said, not brooking any argument: "There's plenty we can do, Bates. I've got a cart and a donkey in the stable, and you can show me the way."

"It's up in the hills, Ma'am. There are Russian patrols all around us. It won't be safe for a lady."

"A fig for your patrols!"

"Yes, Ma'am."

They took her outside and Mahmoud sent the two waiting men off to find another cart or two. And then they began the steep climb back up to the hills together.

She walked close behind them, breathing hard and stumbling once in a while, but refusing Bates help when he offered it. And the first red streaks of the dawn were showing in the eastern sky, turning the green hills to gold and the grass to brilliant copper, when they arrived back at the river.

The men of the Bashi-Bazouk had gone. There were smoldering fires still and there was blood on the ground where Kirk had lain; but of the men, there was no sign.

THE CHARGE OF THE LIGHT BRIGADE

Bates said, "Stone the crows, it ain't even daylight yet, and they've gore."

Mahmoud shrugged. "Of course. In a little while it will be light, you think they stay here in the open?" He looked around, searching the horizon, and said at last, with a kind of definite finality, "There, where the broken rocks are, that is where they will be."

Bates said sourly, "The Inkerman Hills, they'll be thick with Russkies."

Mahmoud shrugged. "If the Russians are there, we will hear my men shooting them." He was already moving off ahead of the cart.

It was a small two-wheeled cart made of hazel saplings, drawn by the smallest donkey Bates had ever seen, a gray-brown, scraggy beast that looked as though it had never seen hay in its life. But it pulled the cart well and strongly on delicate, matchstick legs, even when the wheels had sunk up to their axles in the mud of the river bank. There was a large glass jar of water aboard the cart, and two blankets, and a wicker basket of biscuits, and a piece of salt pork wrapped in a clean cloth, and not much else.

They moved on up the steep slope of Inkerman Hill, and they came across the first sign of their party as the sun came up over the mountain. One guard was waiting there, lying on his belly on the hard red sand and watching for them as they climbed. He got to his feet and looked at the young woman and grinned, and Mahmoud spoke to him angrily and followed him into the tiny gorge where the others had found shelter.

Kirk lay there on some hay they had pulled for him with unexpected solicitude, and one man was with him. The others were out on the hills, standing guard now that the armies could be expected to move again with the light of the day. The young woman went to Kirk and knelt down beside him and looked at the ghastly mess on his shoulder, and when he opened his eyes and stared at her, not believing, she said gently, "My name is Miss Enderly, and I've come to help you."

She was pulling away the rough bandage, the dirty rags, and she shuddered when she saw the wound, and Bates, crouching beside her, said casually, "Not too bad, Ma'am. That's mostly wood ash there."

She said, "There are clean rags in the cart, get them." As he turned to go, she said; "And do you have whiskey? I imagine you do."

He nodded. "Sure, a bottle somewhere."

"Good. Let me have it."

Now Epernon was hurrying in. He had seen her from the post he had taken up on the rocks, and to Epernon all women were beautiful and to be courted, even this scraggly creature with her gawky movements and her torn clothes—the clothes, none the less of a lady. He came up, bowed elaborately, and said:

"May I present myself, Mam'selle? Chevalier Jean-Marie Pierre de la Tour Epernon, *a votre service, chère Mam'selle*..."

Miss Enderly had traveled with her father to many parts of the world, and France was well known to her. She said coldly: "*Chevalier*, did you say?"

Epernon grinned. "Well, soldier, anyway. A great pleasure to see that our ranks have so splendidly been swelled, mam'selle. I trust you will stay with us for a long, long time. We are sadly lacking in the civilized amenities, but I assure you that I will do everything in my power..."

She broke in on his speech, her voice hard and cold: "I have no time now for nonsense. Help me get this mess cleaned up. I need clean water from the cart."

She looked at the great mass of bandages on Kirk's leg, and felt for the broken bones, and watched his face when he flinched—but held his tongue now—and when Bates came back, she said, "How long ago did you set this leg?"

"Last night. I dunno, maybe around midnight. We did a

good job on it."

"Yes, you did. I wish I could say the same for that shoulder. Is there much blood around the breaks?"

"Some."

"A cut, a deep scratch? Or...or just a mess?"

"The bone come through the skin in a couple of places, Ma'am, but we got them back into place again. Yes; he lost a bit of blood there, I'd say."

She sighed. "Then, it will all have to come off."

She began to unwind the bloodied tags, and when the leg was bare she swabbed it with a rag soaked in whiskey, and bound it up again and put back the splints while they watched, and she said to Bates, not taking her eyes off her work and speaking gently now, "Yes, you did a good job with the leg, a very good job."

Gratified, Bates tried to hide his pleasure. He said gruffly, "My ship's the *Arethusa*, Ma'am, just a frigate. We don't carry no doctor on board. A man gets to learn these things."

She said again, "A very good job. In quite a short awhile, if he watches it carefully, the leg will be good again. But if dirt gets into the wound; he'll get gangrene, and then he'll probably die. The rags must always be clean, and disinfected."

Epernon laughed and said, "Clean? Look at us, Mam'selle. We have left cleanliness a long way behind us."

And Bates said, "Shut up, Frenchy, don't you ever know when to keep quiet?"

She turned her attention to the shoulder, and lifted Kirk's head up gently, and said, "I'm afraid that, now, it will hurt more. If you want whiskey to drink...?"

He shook his head, his lips tight. He said, "I can stand it."

"It will be a burning sensation, quite painful. I'm going to disinfect that mess they made of your shoulder, or else you'll be losing an arm. And that wouldn't do now, would it?"

She saw his eyes screw up tight, saw the blood at his

mouth where he bit his lip, but he made no sound. When she had finished, he lay back on the hay and looked at her and said, "How do I say thank you, Ma'am? Is there anything better I can say?"

She shook her head. "No, there's nothing better."

She stood up and handed the whiskey bottle back to Bates and said, "Now I'll take him back with me in the cart."

Bates said stolidly, "No, Ma'am. He's one of us now."

"He comes back with me, Bates."

"No, Ma'am. He stays with us."

Epernon said, smiling gently, "Surely that's for the boy to decide? Whether he wants his own kind for company, or...the delicate pleasures of a woman by his side?"

Bates knelt down beside him and said quietly, "You want to go back to the harbor, Kirk? They'll put you on a ship and send you to Scutari, and in a few months you'll be on your way home again, back to England. Or you want to stay with us?"

Miss Enderly said angrily, "For God's sake, Bates! What use is he to you? Even for your own sakes, how can you lug an injured man around with you? It'll be a week before he can even hobble!"

Not looking at her, Bates said, "Then we'll carry him for a week. In your cart. What's it to be, boy, it's up to you."

Kirk said, struggling, "I don't...I don't want to go to Scutari." The hospital there already had an evil reputation; it was where men were left on the floors to die, without their friends beside them. He said again, whispering, "Don't send me to Scutari, Jack...You're the only friends I've got now..."

Bates stood up. He said firmly, "That's it, Miss Enderly. He stays with us."

She began to argue, but he paid her no attention. He said to Mahmoud, "Go with her, Mahmoud; take her back to the harbor. She can have the donkey and we'll keep the cart."

She tried one last effort, "He'll be of no use to you at all, no possible use!"

Bates said calmly, "Nobody said he would be, Ma'am. But that's not the question, is it? The question is: What does he want to do? And that's already been answered. I'm sorry. And I thank you for what you done."

She turned away sharply to hide her frustration, and Epernon said languidly, "Perhaps I'd better escort her down to Balaklava myself. She won't really be safe with that lustful heathen."

Bates said scornfully, "And with you? Besides, you're a wanted man, Frenchy. They'll clap you in irons in the brig the moment they set eyes on you. Mahmoud takes her. And she'll be safe."

He sat down beside Kirk and began to wipe the dirt off his rifle. He did not look at her again until, riding the tiny donkey with Mahmoud leading, she was well down the slope on her way back toward the tiny squalid village and the sandy road that led to the right-angled inlet from the sea that was Balaklava harbor. Some of the British ships had sailed into the port and tied up at the undefended wharves. It was the lifeline of the army that was soon to lay siege to Sebastopol, ten miles to the northwest.

Among those ships was the luxurious yacht, the *Dryad*, the personal property of Major General the Earl of Cardigan, Commander of the Light Brigade, which friends of his had sailed out from England for him, so that he would not be unduly exposed to the rigors of the campaign and could spend at least his nights in comfort. At this moment, he was taking his bath, having risen early because the weather was fine.

Nine miles away, north of the decrepit little harbor, Kirk, the deserter from Lord Cardigan's forces, lay on his pile of straw and watched the sun moving up over the Inkerman Hills. He heard the distant trumpets and the very faint thud of galloping hooves so he knew that out there somewhere, the Russians were pulling their forces together, regrouping for the defense of

Sebastopol, waiting for the British and the French and the Nizam to hurl themselves once again at their columns.

Waiting, perhaps, for the Bashi-Bazouk as well. He wondered if he would live to fight with them.

CHAPTER 4

This foolish and disastrous war had begun, as most wars do, over a distant squabble that could well have been left to take its own course and seek its own cure.

In Jerusalem, which since 1516 had been part of the Muslim Ottoman Empire of the Turks, the Greek Orthodox Church enjoyed privileges somewhat more considerable than those of the Roman Catholic faith; and there were always bickerings between the priests of the two faiths as to just *who* should be allowed to worship *when* in the Church of the Holy Sepulchre.

Czar Nicholas I of Russia, that foolish and puny man, had somehow arrogated to himself the place of champion of the Christians in the Holy Land, a protector against the Mohammedan zeal of the Turks. But in the Czar's own mind, Christians did not include Roman Catholics, for whom he had nothing but contempt. And Prince Louis Napoleon had similarly taken upon himself the protection of the Catholics, who were his idea of Christians. And when the Catholics wanted keys to the church because the Muslim door keeper was loath to hand them over at the proper times after all, the Greek Orthodox clergy had *their* keys—the squabble inevitably brought Russia and France into confrontation over the privileges of the citizens whose rights they had taken it upon themselves to protect.

The Turks, of course, who held the keys to matter in more ways than one, treated the squabble with the fine Oriental subtlety which it so richly deserved, by agreeing in principle, and then doing nothing whatsoever to implement that principle. This course so enraged Czar Nicholas that he presented the Sultan an ultimatum, backed with a show of force. He moved two army corps to the Turkish frontier. Not to be outdone in these warlike maneuvers and anxious to prove that he could rattle the saber on behalf of his Christians just as loudly as the Czar could to impress the Greeks of the Orthodox Church, Louis Napoleon sent the vanguard of his fleet to the Eastern Mediterranean, and the stage was set.

The Russians promptly crossed the River Prut, then the Russian boundary, and no more doubts could be entertained that war was in the offing, though war had not yet been declared. Indeed, Czar Nicholas sent a circular note to the Powers in Europe, explaining that he was about to obtain satisfaction from Turkey, the "sick man of Europe" as he called it "by force but not by war"—whatever that ambiguous phrase might mean.

And so, on October 23, 1853, Sultan Omar declared a state of war existed between Turkey and Russia, and England and France promptly joined with Turkey, largely because their people at home were thirsting for war. In those far-off days, the civilian population was rarely close to the distant wars of its soldiers, and they expected that troops should feel properly belligerent, as becomes any army.

"Russia," the Czar declared, "is not fighting for material benefit but for the Christian Faith. England and France have allied themselves with the enemies of Christianity, and Russia is fighting for the Orthodox Faith."

The Muslim janitor of the Church of the Holy Sepulchre was able to keep the disputed keys in his pocket, and the war was

THE CHARGE OF THE LIGHT BRIGADE

on.

If the careless maneuvering toward war had taken a long, long time, it was still longer before the shooting would begin. The first troops had left London and Paris in February of 1854, the largest invasion force that history had ever known; but it was not until nearly seven months later at Balchik Bay, fifteen miles north of Varna in Bulgaria, that the Allied force stood ready for the first stage of its action. And now, long before a shot had been fired by either the British or the French—the Turks were holding the Russians at bay and making a very good job of it too—no less than eight hundred British, three thousand Zouaves, and ten thousand Frenchmen succumbed to a virulent outbreak of cholera.

Nonetheless, 57,000 men embarked from Varna for the Crimean coast, though many of their horses and much of their supplies were inadvertently left behind. Although it was the largest expeditionary force that had ever been sent in modern times against an overseas enemy, it was also the least organized and, from the point of view of logistics, the worst managed. The mere loading of the force took a total of ten days; the six thousand packhorses, which had been collected locally with a great deal of difficulty (it was realized how desperately they would be needed in Crimea) were left behind simply because, after all that trouble, there wasn't room for them on the ships; the tents of the men too (though not those of the officers) were abandoned; all the transport carts were left behind (they couldn't get them on board the ships) and no one had even thought of bringing along any medical supplies at all.

On the British side, 24,000 infantry, more than 1,000 cavalry with their mounts, 60 guns and 400 horses to pull them—all were laboriously loaded, and the huge expedition set out on an easterly course. Thirty thousand French troops sailed with them in their own transports, forming for those days, an armada of most impressive proportions.

Headed where? Nobody quite knew.

For it was only at this point that the commanders began to give some thought about where the invasion force was actually going to land. In the British Parliament, it had duly been noted that the Crimea seemed to be a peninsula, so what could be simpler than for the two fleets to sail close inshore at the bottleneck, one fleet on the west and one on the east, where they would be separated by an isthmus a mere ten miles or so across? From this highly strategic position the whole of the Crimea could be effectively cut off. None of the planners seemed to have noted that the water on either side of the isthmus was only three feet deep.

But once the invasion fleets were under way, their lordships began to think about this matter. Lord Cardigan had already scouted the coast and had found a suitable landing-point, but Lord Raglan, his superior and commander in chief of the British forces, was sure he could find a better one. By a fortuitous chain of circumstances he led the fleets to Eupateria where there was, in fact, room for so large a force to land, even though it was under the watchful eyes of a scouting party of Cossacks who sat on their horses on the hills overlooking the beaches and made long and copious notes about the landing operations without any interference whatsoever.

Now, with the troops on shore, was the time when the land transports were sorely needed. In their absence, it was now suggested—the amiable Lord Raglan seldom ordered—that the troops might leave their packs behind too, to save carrying them on the long march—ten days' march at least—to Sebastopol.

So they spent the first night on the beaches without tentage, without greatcoats, without even the most primitive supplies, and in one of the Crimea's vicious rainstorms that soon had the men, barely recovering from the disastrous effects of the cholera epidemic, wallowing in the black wet mud, and shivering in the acute cold.

THE CHARGE OF THE LIGHT BRIGADE

Nonetheless in the morning—after more than a thousand sick men had been carried back onto the ships—the remainder set off jauntily, some 55,000 British and French, on the long march to glory and an end of Russian arrogance. For the ten days' haul they carried three days' rations and almost no water.

History can only raise its eyebrows in surprise that the troops ever got to the River Alma, where the Russians chose to stop them. But they did. And that they passed it and broke the Russian defenses was due entirely to the indisputable fact that the soldier of that day was merely cannon fodder who would march straight into a heavy gun if he were told to, without questioning either the wisdom of his orders or the need for them.

The Russians had stood, though only for a few hours, and the British and French had crossed the river. Nothing now stood the way of their descent upon Sebastopol—now selected at last as the target of the expedition—except the long inlet of water on the north side of the town which was, no doubt, an effective if limited barrier.

Sebastopol was, indeed, the center the Russian forces in the Crimea, but when the advance parties of the British forces reached a point of vantage to the north of the town and within sight of it, it seemed to them that the inlet barrier m might be an insuperable one. A short meeting took place between Lord Raglan and Marshal St. Arnaud—the latter a very sick man now as a result of the epidemic—and it was decided that a frontal attack was impossible. It was decided instead that a flank march should be made to encircle the town and attack it from the south, where there was no water barrier.

And at the precise moment when these august generals were deciding the town could not be taken by frontal assault, the Russian general was deciding it could not possibly he held, and was determining to withdraw the entire Russian army to the east.

It is safe to assume that the next morning, when both armies, each in complete ignorance of the others moves, started on their marches, the only thing that prevented a head-on collision (and no doubt an early end to the war, one way or another) was that the British were late moving off again; they were waiting for the French.

And now, for weeks on end, the two gigantic forces moved around the woods and the plains, the green hills and the dusty valleys of the Crimea, looking for each other and thirsting for battle. Back and forth they moved, sometimes in each other's footsteps, sometimes side by side, and sometimes miles apart. It was a chess game, carelessly played, and the pawns were dying men.

Kirk struggled into a sitting positon, lifted his crutch under his arm, and hobbled over to where Bates was lying by the fire.

He said, "That girl last week, whatever happened to her, Jack?"

Bates shook the ash from his pipe and stretched his long legs lazily. "Ah, that was a pretty one indeed." He took a second thought and said, "Well, not pretty, maybe, but...but if I was thirty years younger, she'd have stirred my blood, Kirk. That she would. A man can't expect the best, not in these heathen parts. He's got to make the best of what he can find."

"What did she say her name was? Enderly?"

"Aye, Enderly. Her father's one of them merchants." Bates rolled over and took a swig of the water bottle, half whiskey, half spirits, it had been a cold night even close to the fire. He said, offering the bottle, "Want some, Kirk?" Kirk shook his head.

Bates said, scratching at his stomach, "You know, seems to me like a strange thing, about them merchants, I mean. They

THE CHARGE OF THE LIGHT BRIGADE

come out on board the same navy that was heading to the Crimea to beat the hell out of the Russkies. We landed them on Russian soil all nice and friendly, and then we pull back and start the bombardment. It don't make sense."

Kirk shrugged. "They're civilians. Fighting's for soldiers, not civilians. You can't expect trade to stop, just because there's a war on, that wouldn't make sense either, would it?"

Bates sighed. "No, I suppose not. But there's a lot in this war that don't make much sense. Not like the old days. I fought under Wellington, did you know that? Lord stone the crows, boy, it was different then." He snorted. "Like that business of leaving half the supplies behind at Varna. If we weren't going to need all that stuff we collected, why did we bring it out from England in the first place?"

Kirk thought for a while. He said at last, knowing he was right, "That's officer business, Jack, it's not for the likes of you and me to question what they decide to do."

"Maybe it's time we *did* question what they do, boy."

It made Kirk feel uncomfortable, this kind of talk. He said awkwardly, "I'll be getting back to the regiment soon. I'm going to miss you, Jack. I never had many friends, and...well you've been good to me, and..." His voice trailed away and he tried his broken leg on the ground and said, "I wonder how long before I'll be able to swing into the saddle again."

"Are you thinking of riding with the regiment again, boy?"

Kirk was surprised. He said, "Of course! What else?"

"What else? I'll tell you what else, Kirk. If it's the good of your country you have in mind, you'll find a better way to serve than with the regiment."

Kirk looked at him, puzzled, and Bates said carefully, "The war's a mess, Kirk, and yet, it's a *just* war. Did you ever stop to think about that? Since I deserted I've done the enemy more damage than I ever did on board the frigate, and my conscience is clear. I'm fighting for the good of my country just as well as I ever did in the Navy." He said with simple dignity, "A man makes up his mind the cause is right, he's got to work for it the best he knows how. And I decided that I could do better on my own, behind the enemy lines, than I ever could with the Navy. The Navy's not what it used to be any more. And neither is the Army. Under the Duke, things were different, but now... So, if you want to join forces with us, you'll find the Bashi-Bazouk are not too bad to fight with, and you'll be a free man."

The young boy was staring at him in something like horror. He said, stammering: "Desert my regiment? Become a..."

"Yes, Kirk, a deserter, like me. They've brought you up to believe that a deserter is the lowest kind of animal there is, but that's only because without their kind of discipline among their troops there's no glory for themselves in it. Have you stopped to consider that?"

Kirk said stiffy: "I'll not have you turning me against my officers, Jack."

Bates shrugged, "It's your own life, Kirk, you have to lead it the way you see it."

"You're making a coward out of me."

"No!" Bates was angry now, but only for the moment. He said sharply, "I came here to fight the enemy and I've killed more of them with my bars hands out here than I ever did on board the *Arethusa*, a good ship though she is!" More gently, he said, "It's not a question of cowardice, but sooner or later a man has to ask himself if what he is being told to do, the way he's being told to fight... if that's the right thing and the right way to do it. It took me forty years to find out that I'd been wrong all along. And you know? That girl who came to take care of you, she was the one made me realize, at last, that I'd done the right thing."

Startled, Kirk said, "Miss Enderly?"

"Aye, your young Miss Enderly." He stood up and turned

to the river bank and said, "Walk with me a ways, Kirk, and I'll tell you."

They strolled together in the early light along the edge of the water, clear again now and running fast, with the wire-strung grapes—what was left of them after the armies had passed through—strung out like green cordons along the scented weeds, grown high now with neglect. They could hear the very distant sound of a bugle call and Bates stopped to listen and said.

"The Russkies, calling the men for morning food."

Kirk said, pressing, "About Miss Enderly...?"

"Aye, your young Miss Enderly." They strolled along, the old man and the young, and Bates said slowly, "There was so much that was wrong on board the ship, the best ship in the Navy, and yet... When the plague hit us, we buried the dead round the clock, no time even for a proper funeral at the end, and we had thirty men lying below with no medicine and no attention because the medicines were all in England, because they said they'd never be needed.

"We sailed out into the deep water, because the officers said that if we got away from the damp breeze that came from the swamps we'd be free of it all, but it only made things worse. We took the cholera out to sea with us, and there, there it killed more than half of our complement. Can you believe that? More than half a ship's company killed at sea by a plague! Only the poor sailors, and I'll tell you why. It was because we were drinking the stinking water they gave us, sour water out of the rivers because there was nothing else to drink. But the officers had their wines, and some of them took sick. And when I told Miss Enderly that we'd sailed out to sea to get away from the cholera, she got angry and said what I'd always suspected, that it had nothing to do with the damn winds at all. And my point, Kirk, is this: They're supposed to look after us, are they not? The officers? But they let us die, and I thought: Jack Bates, after forty years at sea, under their orders, you'll try your hand on your own. You'll be a better man and you'll fight a better war."

"And after forty years you deserted because of that?" There was scorn in Kirk's young voice.

"Not because of that boy. That was just the last straw that broke an old man's back. No, it was the way they treated us, the way they'd always treated us, like cattle, not like men at all! And the way they wanted us to fight this war, like it was a picnic. Do you know that when we left England to land on the shores of the Crimea, there wasn't even a map of the Crimea in the whole God-blasted Navy? Do you know that we got as far as Varna, and the plague, before they even began to worry just where the Russian army might be?"

Kirk said tartly, "They could hardly send spies out."

"Why not? The Russians do, and so do the Turks. And so would the French if they thought we weren't watching them close as hawks. Nobody likes spies, I know that. But that's what we're doing here, we're spying for the Turks, or the British, or the French, or anyone who'll listen to what we tell them." He said morosely, "And that means only the Turks, and they've been fighting better than anyone else so far. We spy, and we hit the Russian patrols and were making a nuisance of ourselves behind their lines. We're doing a job of work and we're free men. And what more can a man ask for than that?"

"But...spying!"

"Aye. If it helps win the war. The Russians do it, so, why shouldn't we?"

"The Russians are the enemy, and there's no reason why we should drag ourselves down to their level, Jack. And the Turks... Well, they're heathens, and we mustn't expect anything better of them. If God had wanted the Turks to behave like Englishmen he'd have made their skins lighter, did you ever think about that?"

"Aye, perhaps you're right, Kirk." But I've fought with the Turk, and, heathen or not, he's not a bad fellow under all that smell and dirt. You've got to admit that it was the Turks who held the Russians back while we were sailing up and down the coast, wondering where we might put near sixty thousand men ashore with no tentage, not enough food, and no water at all except what was in them muddy pools. That's where the plague came from, boy. I'd suspected it all along. And what Miss Enderly said convinced me I was right. I'd done the right thing when I upped and went without a by-your-leave. And I'd do it again if the chance came to me, and now that it's come to you, Kirk, I say desert and be damned to them. Fight this war alongside me and Mahmood, and even Frenchy, he's not a bad fellow either, even if he is a Catholic, and you'll find there's more here to make a man of you than you'll ever find under their orders. Why, do you know that the officers brought their wives out to watch the fighting going on?"

"Yes...yes, I'd heard about that."

Sixty-three army wives had been crowded into the transports at Varma at the very last moment, because they'd made such an unconscionable fuss about being left behind, with no husbands to take care of them. They wanted to see their men in action, and that meant going with them to the Crimea. They had brought along their deck chairs on the crowded transports to make the spectacle less rigorous to watch.

Bates scowled. "The Duke would never have allowed a thing like that. They brought their ladies along to watch us fight and die, like it was a circus for their pleasure."

Kirk said, struggling with the thought, "But they were *officers'* wives, they have certain rights, you know!"

Bates said swiftly, "And us? We don't have no rights?"

"Not many, I grant you that."

"And not enough of them for Jack Bates. And if you're the man I take you for, they won't be enough for you either. Was it your right to be left to die on the battlefield just because all the medicines were forgotten and left behind? Because the only nurses we can get are the men who drink too much to be good soldiers? The habitual drinks used to look after the dying, is that your right too? You'd have died there on that field, Kirk, if me and a handful of stinking Turks hadn't core along to drag you away and make you well again."

Kirk sighed, his anger gone, and his fear too. "Yes, you're right, Jack. Maybe I should listen to you and not to *them*, I dunno."

He hobbled slowly along beside his friend, and Bates said, suddenly sympathetic, "You can't go back till your leg's healed up anyway. So stay with us till then, and...then, we'll see. We do like *they* do. We won't plan anything at all, what do you say, boy?"

Kirk said, "I'll stay with you till my leg's healed, if you'll have me."

"Good, that's settled then. And did you hear the cavalry moving in the night?"

"Aye, I heard it. I wondered if it was my own brigade."

"The Light? No, they was untrained horses, boy, a cavalryman should know that. They were Russians. Mahmoud went up to the top of the rise and took a look. Ten thousand horse, he said, and thirty thousand or more infantry, moving out of Sebastopol."

Kirk frowned. "Away from Sebastopol?"

"Aye. I wondered about that myself."

"Do you think it's fallen already then?"

"No." Bates shook his head firmly. "Not without the sound of the navy guns, we'd have heard them. A flank march, maybe, to turn the British lines as they move south."

High on the hills above them, someone was calling, yelling at them urgently. They swung round to look, and Epernon was running fast down the hill to meet them. He yelled, "Take cover, Cossacks!" and then there was the sound of firing just beyond the brow of the hill.

THE CHARGE OF THE LIGHT BRIGADE

They ran back to the fire, the two of them, and they took their muskets and headed for the shelter of the vineyards, and then a group of horsemen came breasting the hill, tall men on small ponies, with gray overcoats down to their ankles, carrying sabers and lances.

There were eight, ten, eleven of them, sweeping fast down on Epernon as he ran, and he stopped and swung round, dropping to one knee and waiting till they were almost on him before he fired. One of the horsemen fell, and the others swept past him as he jumped quickly and easily to one side and into a gap between two of them. He was running again now, uphill this time, the way he had come, and they saw him pick up the fallen Cossack's lance and stand with it, waiting for the onrush, one man against ten in a demonstration of skill for the watchers below. There was even a grin on his face.

Bates said, aiming his rifle, "Fire when I do, boy, not before." He waited till the horsemen were close on Epernon, saw him throw the lance and leap to one side again, and then they fired. Two men were dropping from their horses, and one of them, his foot caught in the leather stirrup, was dragged screaming rover the rock-strewn grassy ground.

Bates said calmly, "Reload, there's time for another." It took a long time to load the muzzle-loading Minié rifles, to force the bullet down the barrel on top of the clay plug, to hammer it home with just the right pressure so that it would fit tight but still not blow up. Bates' hand moved instinctively while he kept his eyes on the Russians on the hill who were turning now to see where this attack from the rear had come from. Kirk was slower, working with his eyes on his gun. Bates said, "Now, boy, hurry. That's hammered home enough."

The horsemen were turning, beginning to race down the hill. They saw Epernon run from under cover, a Russian smoothbore musket in his hand now, and as he fired they fired too, and two more men fell, and Bates said admiringly, "Good shooting, boy." The range was more than a hundred feet and the guns were not very accurate. The horsemen veered and slewed round, not wanting to charge into the strong wires of the vineyards, and then they were charging off at an angle, yelling their savage cries and giving up the battle nonetheless.

Epernon came running on down the hill, shouting excitedly: "*Tu à vu, mon vieux*? You see how many I killed?"

Bates said, "You missed every one of them, Frenchy. If it hadn't been for me and the boy here..."

"*Eh...regardez-vous la*, take a look over there," One of the Russians was lying with a Cossack lance through his chest, and Epernon said scornfully, "You threw that lance too; maybe?" He clapped Kirk on the back and said, "Nonetheless, for a perfidious English man you are a good man. I like you."

He turned to Bates and said "Two columns of Russian infantry, three miles away to the east, you can see them clearly from the top of the hill. Come, I show you."

Kirk said, "Going to, or coming from, Sebastopol?"

Epernon was surprised. He said, "Yes indeed, a good question and a puzzling answer. They come *from* Sebastopol. And yet, Sebastopol cannot have fallen, we would have heard the sound of the fighting. And can so fine a city fall in so short a time? I do not think so."

"No, it's not fallen, and that's the rear guard moving out," said Bates. "The main forces left in the night. And can you tell me why they should do that? You're a good soldier, Frenchy, tell me what they're up to?"

Epernon said carefully, "If I were General Menshikov, I would leave a holding force in Sebastopol, and I would take the rest of my men out to march east, and north, and west, and south again to hit the Allies in the rear. And at the same time I would attack Balaklava to drive out the ships that are there and cut the Allies off from any further supplies, But Menshikov is a fool. So perhaps he is merely avoiding a battle he thinks he cannot win."

"And the Navy? Where's the Navy, Frenchy?" Bates had not been a freebooter long enough to think that wars could be won without the Navy.

But Epernon only grimaced. "Far out to sea you can see them on the horizon if your eyes are sharp. But which are yours and which are mine, do not ask, my friend, because I do not know."

"Not mine anymore," Bates said, "Where are the rest of the Turks?"

Epernon began to laugh. He said, "They came and took the guns we had hidden from them, and I did not see them, you did not see them, and neither did Mahmoud either. We put the guns there, and they are gone."

The men of the Bashi-Bazouk moved always in the night, in stealth, dike the brigands they were, hiding even from their own kind once the darkness had fallen, the only difference was that if you were on their side they let you sleep, if you were a Russian, they cut your throat.

They climbed steadily, the three of them, Kirk and Bates and Epernon, three lone soldiers in a hopeless war, lost and not even aware of it. They trailed their rifles, and their belts were stuck with pistols and swords and knives, and all hung about with little leather bags full of cartridges for their guns. They had water bottles and pieces of bread and meat wrapped in rags. Of Kirk's uniform, little was left that showed he was once a soldier, and more, a cavalryman of the Light Brigade. His leather crossbelts were scarred and dirty, his jacket torn and patched. He was wondering now if he should find some mutton fat and clean up the leather, and while he wondered about it he pulled off the rag that was wrapped around his head in place of the stiff-peaked cap he had lost and stuffed it in his pocket. It made him feel guilty that he wanted to establish himself as a soldier among them. There a was a stubble of light beard on his face now. Though his shoulder was still painfully stiff and he could not raise his arm above the waist, he could still use both his hands; and if he tried hard, he could hobble along fast enough on his rough-cut crutch—cat from a burned-out wagon shaft with Mahmoud's sharp knife—to keep up with the others, even uphill.

As he walked, he said to Bates, apropos nothing at all, "I wish I knew why they started this war. Can you tell me that, Jack?"

Bates snorted. "Does it matter why? They're Russians we're fighting, ain't they? That's all that matters?"

Kirk laughed suddenly. He said, "You know Lord Raglan, the best soldier the British ever had, next to the Duke, of course, you know what he calls the Russians?"

Epernon was grinning at him, knowing the answer.

Kirk said, "He calls them the *French*, because the only wars he ever fought were against the French, most of his life fighting them. So that's what he calls the enemy now." Mimicking the gentle tones of His Lordship, Kirk said: "May I suggest, my Lords, that we drive the French before us with a frontal assault. The other *French*, under our dear friend, the great Marshal St. Arnaud will attack from the flank till the field is red with French blood: Not the other *French*, of course; they do not shed their blood quite so easily."

Epernon said grimly, "Plenty of our blood has been spilled too, Kirk, do not forget that."

"That St. Arnaud," Bates said. "They say he's a very sick man. The plague, most like, never got over it at Varna."

With sudden anger, Epernon said, "Let him die of it! It was he and his soldiers who killed off my family in Paris. My father, my two brothers, my uncle. The Second Empire, they call it, with Emperor Louis at its head. And how did he get there? He paid St. Arnaud ten thousand francs to massacre every French citizen on the streets of Paris who might have raised his voice in anger at the overthrow of the Republic."

And Bates said gently, "We've all got our reasons, Kirk,

for being here instead of with the troops."

But Epernon was grinning again, his anger quickly gone. "No," he said happily, "I am here because I killed ten Zouaves with my saber, a fight over the just disposition of a captured sword. Which I myself captured, I'd have you know."

"Ten of them...?" Bates asked. "Last time you told it, it was only five."

Epernon shrugged: "Ten, five, what does it matter? As long as you never dispute my competence, we shall remain friends. There..." he pointed. "We climb to the bluff there, and the whole world is laid out for us to see, a world at war below us."

They scrambled over the outcrop of red sandstone, high above the plain they had left, with the gentle river meandering down there far below and behind them, fringed with the ripe greens of the gardens and the vines. Ahead of them, the ground sloped sharply away to the south, dotted here and there with dark green copses and heavy thickets of tall trees and winding dirt roads where a few carts were still being drawn, the stolid peasants ignoring the war that was being fought all around them. Far to the south, the rolling hills stretched to the River Katchka, and on to the Belbek a good day's march beyond it, with another day's march to the Tchernaya, at the mouth of which was the broad saltwater inlet of the Black Sea that was the roadstead for Sebastopol harbor.

To their left, the high Yalta Mountains rose in the east and to their right front, they fancied they could see—or was it only a cloud? —the peaks of Cape Kherson that stood above the tiny harbor of Balaklava.

There, on this little town with its population of a hundred souls, 25,000 British soldiers were soon to descend—for the French, who were following a little way behind, there was no room at all. The generals had not quite realized that thirty mud hut could hardly hold a tentless army of such enormous size.

But now, all was quiet on the rolling plains. And then, coming out of woods some four miles below them, they saw the two columns of Russian infantry that Epernon had spoken of. Their banners flying proudly, the amorphous mass was moving slowly out of the forest into its own pall of dust that reached high in the motionless air as they pounded their feet on the dry roads.

And as they watched, a little way beyond, hidden from the Russians by a fold in the ground, the two Great Divisions of the British Army came into view, marching in the opposite direction on a parallel course, a great solid mass of soldiery in square formation, four squares spread out across the plain in their scarlets and blues, their gold and silver, their high bearskins and peaked shakes, their pipe-clayed webbing white in the morning sun, their brasses shining and their bayonets glistening. Behind them, the French Army now appeared, marching in their habitual diamond formation, with one division in the van, one in the rear, and one on either flank.

The Allies were less than a mile away from the Russians as the two forces marched, each in its own direction, across the plain. But for the fortuitous circumstances of the gentle rise in the ground that hid each from the other's view, they would have heard each other's pounding footsteps.

Bate stared. From high up here on the mountain, it was like looking down on a sand table, with 55,000 British and French, and 45,000 Russians countermarching there below; neither of them knew of the others presence; nor had either of them any idea of the enemy's strength.

Bates said, "Stone the crows, look at 'em!"

Kirk scowled and said, "The Russians are as bad as our lot if they can let that happen. Do you think they know where they're going? Either of them?"

Epernon said mildly, "It is strange how the British always use the square formation when they don't know where the enemy is."

THE CHARGE OF THE LIGHT BRIGADE

They sat down on the red rocks, the three of them, and watched the armies down there for an hour. And, at last, the Russian columns moved into the trees again and were gone; and soon, a fold in the ground hid the rest of the troops from view, and the plain was empty again, with only the solitary carts bumping along behind their swaybacked donkeys, a few peasants, plodding amiably along, and thin wisps of blue smoke from cottage fires rising up and hanging there, and the dotted greens and browns and neat squares of farmland.

And all was silent, and gentle, and full of an impossible peace.

CHAPTER 5

The British had landed the guns from the ships, the heavy guns on tiny wooden wheels that were perfectly adequate for rolling over the ships smooth decks but less so on the deeply rutted dirt roads of the Peninsula, the ancient Crim Tartary.

And now that the Russian Army had abandoned Sebastopol, the Russian Navy had sunk seven of its ships across the mouth of the harbor, in case the British should try a seaborne assault. And the shipless sailors had, per force, landed in the town to organize some sort of defense now that the great army had deserted them. They would have been alone except that three thousand of the troops Menshikov had withdrawn, under one General Moller, somehow got lost—even the Russians had no maps of the area and after marching all day, incredibly, found themselves back at the point from which they started, in Sebastopol.

Had the British attacked at this point instead of marching about so hopelessly—at one point, the advance party had turned *left* at a fork in the road, and the following main body had tuned *right*—it is possible that the whole of the Crimea would have fallen in a matter of hours; and the war would have been quickly over. But soon, General Menshikov decided that his earlier decision had been a wrong one, and that he ought, perhaps, after all, to have left at least a garrison in the town. So he promptly sent back 25,000 more of his men, though he kept his main forces well out of the way. It is possible that the astonishing defeat at the Alma, where Allied stupidity had been overcome only by the individual, if somewhat automated, courage of the troopers, had taught him a salutary lesson about the fighting abilities of his own forces. So far, whenever he had met the British, or the French, or the Turks—particularly the Turks—his casualties had been very heavy.

So at this point, Sebastopol, once nearly deserted at a time when the Allies decided they should *not* attack, was strongly defended by over 28,000 assorted fighting men, now that the Allies had decided that they *should* attack.

And now, moreover, a singular circumstance had come about. Though Their Lordships had once decided to cut off the whole of the Crim Tartary from reinforcement by straddling the neck of the isthmus, it was now apparent that the defenders had absolute and easy access to the whole of Russia since all the attackers were south of the town and had left the northern approaches entirely unprotected. So the "siege," as it was hopefully called, was not a siege at all, the defenders were able to come and go, with supplies or with wounded, as they pleased.

Nonetheless, now that the Allies were in what they firmly believed was a good position to attack the town, the British land forces under Lord Raglan, with the French land forces under St. Arnaud, together with their respective fleets, all began a concerted bombardment of the forts protecting the town. It does not seem to have occurred to them that on the north—the north which had seemed to them so strongly held—there were virtually no defenses, while on the south, which they were now hitting, strong forts had been built to withstand just the type of naval assault they were now attempting. The forts were well built and facing south, and the attack was quite obviously not going to be the easy walkover that the commanders envisaged.

There was a little trouble too with the fleets. It had been decided that the joint sea-land bombardment would start at six-thirty in the morning, and only later did the fleets—without informing the land forces decide that they would not leave their anchorages at the mouth of the Katchka River, some twelve miles north, until eight o'clock. And then, the French decided that instead of sailing past the forts while firing, as had been agreed, they would anchor and fire from the stationary position. Unhappily, they chose to anchor directly in the British line of fire, a fact that created no little confusion.

On that sunny morning of October 17, 1854, the assault on Sebastopol, for which the troops had left their homes a trifle over eight months before, did actually begin by land and by sea. It was the wrong time and from the wrong direction but it did actually begin.

In spite of the difficulties of maneuvering the heavy guns cover the broken terrain, the British had succeeded in setting up two batteries totaling seventy-three guns—all in full view of the enemy. The French had placed fifty-three guns on a ridge of land they named Mount Rodolph. And during the day, these guns between them fired more than 8,500 assorted projectiles into the town killing eleven hundred of the forty thousand defenders— military and civilian. They, in their turn, hurled back twenty thousand cannonballs and shells—most of the gunners were sailors and thought in terms of naval broadsides—and killed two hundred of the attackers. In the late morning, a chance Russian shot landed on the French ammunition depot on Mount Rodolph and blew it up, and fifty men were killed. Whereupon the French general courteously suggested that the artillery might now withdraw, which it promptly did, and the French share of the fighting was ended. It was a little after half-past ten in the morning.

The British guns continued to fire, and in the middle of

the afternoon succeeded in blowing up a Russian ammunition depot, creating a wide breach in the defenses which now should have been stormed by the infantry.

But, while the plans for the assault were being formulated, Their Lordships had quite forgotten to stipulate at what time the infantry should go in. There was the breach waiting for them, but no plans had been made to exploit it. Indeed, even if plans *had* been made, it would have been politic to abandon them now that the French had withdrawn from the fighting.

So, at the end of the day, the battle was called off. The breach was repaired, and the day's assaults had left the town virtually unscathed and still firmly in the hands of the defenders. The following morning, the London newspapers arrived at the end of their long, slow haul from England. They contained the somewhat premature announcement that Sebastopol had been captured by the ever-victorious Allies.

The sound of the guns had been rolling over the plain all day.

Bates said, "That's the *Arethusa* firing, I'll be bound."

There were sixty-eight of the Bashi-Bazouk gathered now on the western slopes of the Inkerman Hills, overlooking the hillock the French called Mamelon that was later to be the setting for the worst French tragedy of the war and at the same time one of their greatest victories. But that would be later, after St. Arnaud had died and the command had passed, at last, to the tough and ambitious General Pelissier, a man made of stronger fiber.

These were the men of the commando of Bashi-Bazouk to which Bates and Epernon had attached themselves. There had been more than two hundred of them less than a week ago, but repeated brushes with the enemy, whom they scorned as infidels, had reduced their number by more than two-thirds. They rode and fought like devils, and they feared nothing in this world or the next. There were infidels to kill with the unaccustomed blessing of their government, and loot to be found on the fields, and women to be taken in the villages, and death would carry them straight to Paradise which Allah had reserved for those who died in a Holy War. They wore brightly colored rags, they carried an odd assortment of ancient weapons, and they had no discipline at all, but they were a deadly menace behind the Russian lines.

There were horses champing at the grass, the short, stubby ponies that had come from as far afield as Kurdistan, with brightly decorated saddlecloths, and beaten brass on their leather; tough, thick-legged ponies with shaggy hair and sudden, nervous movements. The men who rode them were camped around an open fire, with the guards, as always, on the highest points, eating their goat meat and drinking the sour wine they had taken from the villages below. The air was heavy with the sweet smell of coffee and cardamom, and two of them, watched by a dozen of the others, were fighting, rolling over and over on the dry sandy earth and each trying to ram his knife into the other's neck.

Bates had come to regard them as his comrades, though they came and went at will, and usually at night. They would lie by the fires when the moon rose, and when the sun came up they would be gone again, and only the sound of distant shooting would tell of their whereabouts. He fought with them, and spied with them, and sometimes gave them orders and he had come to love them. He turned now at the sound of the cheering and jeering and walked over leisurely to where the men were fighting. He watched for a while and then suddenly shot out a foot and kicked at a knife-hand, then drove his foot squarely into a bearded face, and when one of the men yelled and came at him, enraged at this infidels interference, he shouted, "Enough!" and hit him hard on the jaw with his fist. The man went sprawling, and suddenly Mahmoud was there, placing himself firmly between them and saying, "We fight Russians, not each other."

Bates shrugged. "Just what I was about to explain to them, friend."

Mahmoud had returned from a scouting sortie, and he went over to the fire with Bates and pulled a leg from a roasting goat, pulling at the tough meat with his sharp teeth, the fat running down over his bearded chin. He waved the bone toward the top of the hill and said, "To the south, a patrol of infantry, fifty, sixty men I think we kill them soon." He chewed on the meat, and Bates nodded and said, "Good, it's time we had a fight again."

Kirk was there, hobbling over to talk to them. He said eagerly: "A fight?" And Bates turned to him: "Not for you, Kirk boy, not yet awhile."

Kirk said, "Give me a horse, and I'll ride. Give me a gun, and I'll shoot. You'll see."

Bates grinned at him, "Not yet," he said again. "You're half a man still and half a man can't ride with the Bashi-Bazouk."

Astonishingly, he was a good rider himself, Bates. He swung himself up onto his horse and sat there, looking down at the boy and grinning, and said: "Even a sailor can ride better than a man with only one leg."

Kirk said, smiling; "Where did you learn to sit a horse like that, sailor? On board the *Arethusa*?"

Bates laughed. "When I was a boy, when I was nine years old, I was looking after the Squire's horses when my father died. I took good care of them too, a string of the finest hunters a man could ever hope to see. But the Squire was a bad man, he used to beat me, and so...so, one day I ran away and joined the Navy. It's not hard to get back into the saddle, not even after all these years with sea legs."

Mahmoud was laughing. Bates' long legs dangling over

the tiny horse's back reached almost to the ground. He leaped up onto his own pony and yelled an order, and suddenly there were men running from the fire and stepping up, it seemed into their saddles, wheeling their horses, and raising their rifles high in the air, their bright rags fluttering, and yelling their savage war cries. And then, they were gone, the dust flying up under their horses' hooves, the sound of them loud in the cool air.

Kirk watched them go a trifle sadly and hobbled slowly up the hill toward the top. In a little while, he threw down his crutch and continued, limping, with his broken leg taking his weight, grimacing with the pain and feeling the tears coming into his eyes, fighting them back. He found Epernon squatting under the shade of a rock, his rifle cradled in his arms, and the Frenchman looked up and smiled and said, "It is good to see you without the crutch. Throw it away, my friend, you will learn to do without it. Crutches are only for the very old, or for the very lonely."

Kirk shook his head and sat down painfully beside him. He worked his right arm in little circles, feeling the numbing sensation still in his shoulder, and he said, "You see? I can use the arm again. They're a rough crowd, aren't they?"

Epernon raised an eyebrow. "The Bashi-Bazouk? Yes, they are rough. But they are good soldiers, the best there are. They fight like devils, each man for himself and to hell with the others."

They were a government force, these brigands, armed and encouraged by the Sultan, but not maintained by him. They received no pay, no food, no comforts, nothing but the assurance that they were fighting a Holy War against the infidel Russians (with the infidel French and British lending a helping hand once in a while). They supported themselves, living off the land, taking what they needed at the point of a gun or a sword, reigning over the territory they worked in by the force of the terror they inspired. Sometimes, it was even necessary for the regular Turkish Army to make forays against them and to disarm them, whenever their excesses passed the point of tolerance. They moved in the night like silent animals, and they killed by stealth; and by day, they flaunted the sharpness of their blades and the strength of their arms and were a terror to anyone whose path they crossed.

They were riding now, more than fifty of them, in the distance, down the steep slope of the southern cliff heading for the forest below where the patrol had been seen. The rest, those too seriously wounded to ride, had been left behind, without orders, to guard the camp.

Watching them, Kirk said, "It makes my heart heavy, you know that? To see them riding off together."

Epernon said softly, "Together... Do you miss your old friends so badly?"

"No, it's not that. To tell the truth, in my crowd I never had many friends. But...yes, together is the word."

"You're one of us now, Kirk."

"Maybe."

There was a soft whistle behind them and, when they looked round, one of the guards was there, standing on one leg and leaning on a stick (his right foot had been sheared off by a Russian saber). He was pointing to the east, not attempting to take cover, Epernon got to his fest and said, "I'll take a look. Stay here, Kirk."

He took his rifle and ran quickly up the slope and stood there, looking down past the Mamelon toward the Woronzoff road, the dirt track that led all the way to Yalta, twelve miles to the southeast. He turned in a moment and shouted something that Kirk did not understand and waved his arm in a signal, calling. Kirk struggled to his feet and limped painfully up the hill, looking back once and wondering if he should go and collect his crutch and deciding against it. He hobbled up to Epernon and looked down.

There was a small handcart being pulled by a large and rough-haired dog, and a woman was walking along beside it. Epernon grinned and said, "You see who it is, Kirk?"

But Kirk had seen. He was already hobbling down the slope toward the road, and Epernon stood there watching him, his eyes bright and his white teeth showing as he laughed to himself.

Kirk yelled at the top of his voice, the sound of it carried on the breeze to the tiny figure far below. "Miss Enderly! Miss Enderly! It's me, Kirk...!"

Far away, a tiny white speck in the distance, she turned to look. She spoke to the man who was with her, a stubby, sturdy figure with a rifle cradled in his arms, and ran up the hill to meet Kirk as he hobbled down toward her.

When they came together, she held out her hand to steady him and said reprovingly, "No crutches? Surely they can make your some."

He held out his hand to her, his face suffused with pleasure. He said shyly, "I never did thank you for what you did for me, did I?"

She took his hand, held it, and said, shaking her head; "No thanks are needed. What did you say your name was?"

"Alexander Kirkaldy, Miss Enderly. They call me Kirk; it's easier."

"Well, Kirk... I'm glad to see you on your feet, even though you should be in a hospital. Have they treated you well, those savages?"

"They are not savages, Ma'am, they're good men. And, yes, they've treated me well. Thank you, Ma'am."

She laughed. "And don't call me Ma'am! My name's Jenny."

"Jenny?"

"Jenny."

They stood there for a moment, still holding hands,

listening to the guns. A little embarrassed at his silence, she took her hand from his and said, "And will you be going back to your ship soon?"

"No ship, Ma'am...Jenny. That's Bates. I'm a cavalryman."

Under the dirt and grime, his brightly colored uniform was falling apart, turning into red-grimed rags. As though suddenly conscious of it, he began to brush away some of the top layer of dirt.

She smiled. "Ah yes, of course, the Lancers, isn't it?"

"Yes Ma'am, Jenny. And we don't all look like this."

"No, of course not. And Bates is the sailor. Is he still with you?"

"Yes, Jenny, he is."

"And you're both deserters now."

He hesitated: "Yes. Yes, I suppose I am too. But... Well, I haven't made up my mind yet. Maybe I'll go back, and maybe I won't."

"Are you tired of the war, like the rest of us?"

"No, it's not that..." Wanting to change the subject and suddenly aware of the danger for her, he said urgently, "But you shouldn't be out here so far from...from wherever it is you're supposed to be!"

The sound of the guns was appalling now. They could clearly see the columns of smoke rising over the near ridge beyond which Sebastopol lay.

She said, frowning, "There's more danger for them down there, near the town. The Allies have got the Russians penned in Sebastopol, they can't get out. There's terrible fighting going on."

Kirk said, "In the town? Not all of them. There's another forty or fifty thousand men on the other side of the hills." He pointed back behind them. "Over the Inkerman Hills, down in the woods there somewhere, forty or fifty thousand Russkies, cavalry and infantry, artillery too."

Her frown deepened. "It can't be so, Kirk! Surely you're wrong."

"No Ma'am. We saw them. We saw the British army too, and the French, all of them marching and countermarching. You get high enough up on these hills you can see everything, all laid out below you. You can see Sebastopol too, from the very top. And what a mess they're making of it!"

She sighed. "Yes, they say it'll fall by the end of the day, but... Well, I don't know. The French have stopped fighting, they gave up this morning when their ammunition depot blew up."

"So that's what it was. We heard it, Jenny, we thought maybe it was that Russian fort, what's its name?"

"Fort Constantine? No, Fort Constantine's not been touched, it's too strong for the guns."

"Oh. Then maybe the Fleet's taken the harbor at least? Bates said they'd be in the roadstead now, firing broadsides at the defenses."

"No, not that either. The Russians have sunk their ships across the harbor mouth."

"Then if they can't reduce the fort and they can't get into the harbor...it's not much use, Jenny, is it?"

"No, Kirk, it's not. And, to tell the truth, it never was."

"And you still shouldn't be out in the open here. Would you mind telling me where you're going?"

"Back to the harbor at Balaklava."

"Balaklava? What's in the harbor there?"

She was surprised: "Didn't you know? That's where the Fleet's headquartered."

"No. No, I didn't know that. We've been moving east, keeping away from the coast, keeping up on the mountains. That's where the Bashi-Bazouk like to be, always, up in the hills where there are valleys to hide in when the going gets rough."

"And the Ninety-third Highlanders are camped in the

THE CHARGE OF THE LIGHT BRIGADE

plain around the village, you didn't know that either?"

"The Ninety-third?" Kirk was frowning, trying to piece together all the limited knowledge he had of tactics. "That's not much more than five hundred men, and there's forty, fifty thousand Russians all around them, do they know that?"

"There are a thousand Turks with them, and a field battery too, I believe, but... No, Kirk, the Russian Army is in Sebastopol, or else why are we bombarding it all day long?"

Kirk said glumly, "You tell me that, Jenny. I just don't know enough. I'm not..." He hesitated, ashamed of his ignorance. "I'm not a man with any learning, Jenny, I didn't have too much schooling. I always had an officer to tell me what to do. But now, now I've seen the way my new friends fight, it seems to me that maybe I ought to know more, myself, of what's going on. Is that a bad thing to believe?"

"No. No, Kirk, it's a very good thing."

"The Lord's chosen to make an ignorant man of me. He must know what He had in mind for me."

"Perhaps. But He never said you mustn't try to improve yourself." She said impulsively: "Come with me now, Kirk, come with me to Balaklava. What did you say your unit was?"

"The Light Brigade, Jenny, the Seventeenth Lancers."

"Then we'll find where they are and you can go to them, and..." She broke off, seeing the tightening of the lines at his mouth.

He said, "Not before I see my friends again, Jenny. Jack Bates has gone off with the Bashi-Bazouk to attack a Russian patrol. He wouldn't like it if I wasn't here when he came back."

She said, pleading: "Bates is a confirmed *deserter*, Kirk, you mustn't allow him to influence you so much! For you there's still a chance, you're wounded and you can tell them you planned to rejoin them all along..."

"But I didn't, Jenny, and that would be a plain lie. To tell the truth, I didn't plan to desert them either, but...well, I just haven't made up my mind yet."

"But you said you were tired of the war!"

"No. No, I didn't say that. Maybe I'm tired of the way it's being fought, and..." He frowned. "How can they leave the Ninety-third in that valley down there, with no protection at all? Even *I* know that that doesn't make much sense! There are hills all around them, and the Russians are out in the open and mobile. It just doesn't make any kind of sense at all!"

Jenny said gently: "The Alma didn't make much sense either, Kirk. But that was a great and glorious victory."

Kirk smiled quickly, his boyish face showing a sudden humor. "Aye, it was, once the officers stopped giving out their orders and we took things into our own hands. When we charged that redoubt, there was only General Codrington and that Colonel Lacy Yea shouting view-hullos at us, racing up and down as if they were at a fox hunt. But the fighting... Old Cod pointed his sword and charged, and he left us to do what was natural, and we took that redoubt without any orders at all. That's the way a war should be fought. Not...not like this."

There was the sound of a great explosion across the ridge, and a dark column of smoke arose above it. They turned to watch, and Kirk said urgently, "If the main force of the Russians moves in to relieve Sebastopol, they'll pass this way, and it won't be very safe in these hills, Jenny. You'd best be getting back."

Frowning, she said, "Have you sent word to the Allies, about the Russians out there? If it's true? They think they're all bottled up in the town."

He said glumly, "Aye, we sent word, but the messenger was just kicked in the behind and told to be on his way. I wish you'd go now, it's not safe for you here."

Her head was held very high, "And you won't come with me?"

He looked down to where the dogcart was standing, the

stolid peasant waiting there, a long Turkish musket held by the barrel now across his broad shoulder. He asked her, "Your guard?"

"Yes. They gave me one of the irregulars. I'm taking medicines to the field hospital, they've nothing there at all, no bandages, no medicines, no disinfectants...no beds, even. The wounded are lying on the ground under stifling hot tents and dying."

She turned away and turned back to him when he said:

"You see? It's not the way to fight a war, I know it."

For a long time she held his look. She said at last, more gently, "You must make up your own mind, Kirk. But don't settle too deeply into the role you've chosen. There's still time, there'll still be a little more time perhaps, but not much. If you're away too long..."

"I know, Jenny. I know what I have to do."

"That's just it, you don't. But when you make up your mind, please try and think hard about it, will you promise me that?"

"Aye, that much I'll promise. I'm not a man to make up his mind too quickly, not to anything. Where are you camped? In Balaklava?"

"No," she pointed to a long low hill, covered with yellow gorse and dotted with small stands of hazel trees, "there, beyond the rise, there's a farmhouse, Tulan's farm, they call it. Only it's empty now, nothing there but dead sheep in the fields."

"Will I see you again?"

"If you come back to us you will."

"I wish I could, Jenny, just for that alone."

She blushed, the crimson suffusing her pale white skin, and turned away. He stood there for a long time, watching her slight figure move down the hill. And when she reached the cart in the distance, he was still watching her as she waved once and set off.

He sat down on the grass to watch till she had disappeared. And the, seeing the bright refection in the sand, he stared, and moved over and picked up a small gold medallion she had dropped, its fragile chain broken. He wondered if he should hurry after her with it, and then he decided to keep it till the next time they should meet.

The next time, he was thinking, and the thought gave him pleasure. He got up, and began moving slowly up the hill again, climbing to where Epernon was waiting for him.

Epernon put a hand on his shoulder and said, "I'm glad she didn't convince you to go back, Kirk."

Kirk looked at him sharply and said nothing.

CHAPTER 6

Bates and the others returned when night was falling.

He had set out with fifty men, and returned with twenty-one. But he was in high spirits. He said, galloping up to Kirk, "A good fight, boy, we killed more than half of them." It did not seem to worry him that more than half his own men had been killed as well.

They were carrying one of their number across the saddle of a led horse, a huge giant of a man who was called Suleiman el Kebir, the Big One. The blood was still pulsing out of his huge body, soaking into a dozen crude bandages that had been tightly bound around his chest and his legs and his arms. Mahmoud dragged him from the saddle and lowered him to the ground, and said indifferently: "He get better, is my cousin, a strong man..."

And with them was a prize catch, a Russian colonel, a lieutenant, and a sergeant. Their hands were bound tightly behind their backs, and there were ropes round, their necks, tightly knotted, that joined one to the other as they stumbled along behind the ponies.

Almost all the men were wounded to one degree or another. Mahmoud had taken a saber-cut across his chest that had laid open the rib cage, and there was a new scar running across his face where the point of a lance had just missed his forehead and gone scouring across his cheek.

Bates was unhurt, and he dropped off his horse beside Kirk and sank to the ground, and said wearily, "The way they ride... Sometimes I wish I was back on board the *Arethusa*." He brightened quickly, "But not for long, boy." He said again, "It was a good fight."

Kirk said, "The patrol?"

Bates jerked a thumb at the captives. "That's a good prize to bring home, and the others...forty, fifty, maybe more of them dead, and the rest running fast for home. We fought the way a man is supposed to fight, quick in and quick out, short and sharp and soon over, with us riding off with their weapons and their colonel."

Three of the Turks were piling the captured rifles, the smoothbore rifles with no accuracy or range that the Russians used, sorting out the best of them, stacking the cartridges up on the rocks in little heaps, sharing them out. One of them put aside his looted Minié, took up one of the new weapons, examined it briefly, then threw it down in disgust, and took up his own gun again. Some men were carrying logs and building up the fire.

Epernon murmured something that Kirk did not hear; was it in French? And Bates looked at him and nodded and got up once more and said to Kirk, "Show me how you can walk on that leg, boy."

He led him away, past the Russian prisoners. Kirk looked at them curiously, the first time he had seen the enemy so close. Just men like me, he was thinking. The sergeant was an old and grizzled man, with shaggy white hair and a dark, passionate face, with yellow moustache and white beard, and black, black eyes that now were stolid and seemingly lifeless. The colonel, a tall thin man with a crude bandage over his head, was holding his nose in the air as though smelling the scent of these savages and not liking it at all. There was almost a look of amused contempt on his bright, alert face. The lieutenant could not have been much older than Kirk, and his eyes were red and sore in a pale, drawn face; he was trembling.

Bates took his arm as he hesitated and pulled him away gently, and Kirk said, "What will happen to them, Jack? Why did you bring them here?"

Bates said, "Not me, boy. The others. I'd have left them out there to find their own way home; the fight's gone out of them anyway. But the others... No, you can't argue with a Turk when it comes to prisoners."

Insisting, Kirk "And what will happen to them now?"

Bates hesitated. "They'll be killed now."

There was a little silence. Kirk said at last, very quietly, "They should have been killed out there when the blood was hot. It's not good to kill in cold blood; not even prisoners. Not even Russians."

"Aye, maybe you're right. I don't like it too much myself, but... It's war, Kirk, that's all there is to it."

Kirk was holding back, and Bates took him firmly by the arm and said, "It's not for the likes of us, Kirk, to watch what they do."

"And so, we turn our backs. Is that what you're saying?" The boy was angry now, savagely angry.

"Aye, that's what I'm saying. We turn our backs." Bates said vehemently, showing his own shame. "What do you want me to do? Tell two score of the Bashi-Bazouk to let them go? They'd cut our own throats if we tried to stop them."

"Then tell Mahmoud."

"Mahmoud too! He's no less a heathen just because he speaks a few words of a civilized tongue. We'll leave them alone, Kirk! They know what they have to do and there's no power on earth can stop them from doing it!"

"If you won't do something, Jack, then I will!" Kirk tried to turn back, but Bates' grip on his arm was a steel vise, pulling him away. Bates called out angrily, "Frenchy!"

The Frenchman came running, and Bates said, milder now, "Come with us, Frenchy, the boy wants to go back and upset their plans."

Epernon looked grim, unaccustomedly grim. He took Kirk's other arm and said slowly: "Kirk, my friend, you've seen men die in battle, you've seen them lying on the field with their bodies on fire, you've seen them mutilated and cut to pieces, you've heard their screams, Well, isn't that what we joined the army for, to cut men to pieces because they're our enemies? Is it better to kill them when they're fighting than it is when they've given up? Is the hatred gone just because they raise their arms and surrender? That's just a convention, my friend, that's supposed to separate us from these savages, that's supposed to make us civilized while they're just...heathens. But if you've no taste for it, why then turn away from it and pretend it isn't happening." He said sardonically, "You and I will let the prisoners live to fight again. We'll leave the Turks to follow their desires too. And then we'll ask ourselves who makes the better soldier." He spread his arms in a gesture, a smile on his thin, handsome face. "There, I've washed my hands of them. You see how easy it is?"

Kirk said furiously, "How easy it is to become a savage?"

Epernon clapped him on the back and said, "Yes, my friend, exactly that. Can we be good Christians and go to war? Of course not! So let us enjoy the state of savagery that war has forced upon us. There's little else we can do."

It was useless to argue.

Kirk allowed himself to be dragged away, and in a little while, as they found shelter in a secluded gully, with the darkness all around them now and the moon just coming up over the top of the high Fedioukine Hills to the north of the Woronzoff road, Epernon said, trying to take their minds away from what was going to happen, or already happening now

THE CHARGE OF THE LIGHT BRIGADE

behind them:

"The beautiful Miss Enderly was here today, Jacques."

Bates said, surprised, "The nursing lady?"

"Yes, the nursing lady. She paid us a social visit."

Bates looked at Kirk, and Kirk said glumly, knowing his present battle was lost:

"The Fleet's in Balaklava harbor. And the Highlanders are camped out in the plain there, with the Russians all around them, five hundred horsemen and some Turks against the whole of the Russian Army."

Bates scratched his head, "Balaklava? I was in there once, not room there for more than two, three ships, four at the most."

Kirk shrugged: "That's what she said." He looked up at Bates and said, challengingly, "She wanted me to go back with her and find my unit." Bates did not answer, and Kirk said at last, sulking, "I told her I couldn't go without first letting you know."

"If that's what you've decided to do, boy."

Kirk said angrily, "I've not made my decision. And don't call me boy."

Sitting on the hard ground, rocking back and forth on his haunches and lighting his pipe with a touchwick, blowing on it to make the wick glow, Bates said mildly, "I'm old enough to be your grandfather, Kirk, and to me you're just a boy. But if it pains you, I'll not use the word again."

There was a long, uneasy silence. It was broken by a sudden scream back there, and Kirk felt Bates' hand tighten on his wrist.

Nobody spoke. They could smell the fires here, the fires from behind them and the fires from the town below, which cast, above the ridge, a pale red glow in the sky. The bombardment had long since come to an end, and the night was silent and cold, with a cool breeze blowing off the sea. Kirk looked round to the south where, he was sure, the main body of the Russian Army was moving still, searching out its enemy and not knowing where to look for them. It occurred to him that they must be thinking that the attack on Sebastopol was no more than a diversion, or they'd be moving in to its relief; or perhaps they were, at this moment, doing just that?

He said, worrying, "Those columns we saw yesterday, a mighty strong force, why don't they march on Sebastopol and take our troops in the rear? Can you tell me that, Jack?"

Bates shrugged. "Perhaps they're doing that now, Kirk. Perhaps that's why the Highlanders are in the plain there, to keep an eye out for them. St. Arnaud's a fool, and Ragland's a clown, so perhaps they don't even know what they're letting themselves in for." He added glumly, "And the admirals are not much better, either, even if they are in the Navy. I wonder who's aiming the guns on the *Arethusa* now? My gunners mate was just a kid, not much older than you, Kirk, but a good man. He'll be master gunner now, I'm thinking."

Now there was that scream' again, long-drawn-out this time and piercing, not stopping, but continuing horribly to echo into the moonlit night. Bates put out a hand to Kirk, but the boy pushed him away and struggled to his feet, pulling himself up by the rocks and moving away. Epernon reached out to stop him, and. Kirk hit him hard on the side of the face and knocked him down. Bates withdrew his hand and stared, and then Kirk was stumbling back the way they had come, heading for the fire, its light much brighter now, falling down as the pain in his leg hit him, and pulling himself up by the strength of his will and hobbling on with the blood pounding in his damaged shoulder:

And when he reached the fire, he forced his way through the ring of silent when who were gathered there and pulled up short in horror. The sergeant and the colonel were stretched out dead on the ground, their naked bodies covered with blood; and the young lieutenant, fully clothed and bound, was rolling on the fire while three of the Turks held him there with long poles. His flesh was on fire.

THE CHARGE OF THE LIGHT BRIGADE

Kirk screamed and threw himself forward and dragged the body out from the flames, and then a rough hand took him and pulled him to his feet and thrust a long knife under his chin, and the grinning face was Mahmoud's.

Mahmoud said, "Nothing you can do, woman." He thrust Kirk away from him brutally, throwing him down over the body of the young lieutenant. The screaming had stopped now, and the air was filled with the sweet stench of smoldering flesh. Kirk rolled over on his stomach, the pain gripping him bodily, and looked into the young dead face and vomited.

He heard the sound of Turkish laughter, deep and guttural and filled, somehow, with anger. And then Bates and Epernon were there, pulling him once more to his feet and leading him away, and Epernon was holding out the crutch that had once been thrown away, holding it out to him and saying gently, "Too soon, Kirk, too soon, use the crutch, it will be easier for you."

Kirk said angrily, thrusting him away, "I do not need a crutch. I don't need either of you! Murderers!"

They stood back, both of them, and left him standing there, swaying, trying to find his balance. Bates said very quietly:

"Yes, Kirk, were murderers, all of us. But that's what this war is, isn't it? The fire's no more than a lance through the belly, or a sword in the gut, or a red-hot cannonball in the chest. Is it now?"

Kirk raised his eyes to them and looked at them long and steadily. They were friends, and he knew it. He took a deep breath and said at last, very low:

"I've been looking for an answer, Jack, searching for a long time now. And now, perhaps I've found it."

He turned and limped away. He walked up the hill for a long time, and when the pain became unbearable, he dropped to all fours and crawled, and he did not once look back at them, knowing that they were still there, his friends, staring after him as he moved farther and farther away from them.

At last, he came to a patch of sweet green grass, and he turned over and lay on his back and stared up at the moon. He bit his lip to drive away the pains in his leg and his shoulder, and touched his arm to see if the blood had broken through; and at long last, his eyes wet, he fell into a restless sleep.

And in the morning, long before the others were awake, he found his crutch again and slowly moved off, alone, down into the valley.

He was not even sure which way he was going.

Balaklava, Jenny Enderly had said, and he knew that the tiny town was on the coast to the south, over the brow of the long ridge they called the Causeway, and below the high peak of Cape Kherson, which stood up against the autumn sky like a sentinel.

It was as though a great load had dropped from his shoulders. When he thought about Jack Bates, it was with a deep regret for the parting, even with Frenchy too, but he was sure that he was doing the right thing at last.

He stopped for a while in a wooded copse, where the scents were strong and the birds were singing loudly, and he ate some of the old meat he had brought with him—a habit he had picked up from the Turks, never to travel without meat in his pocket—and lay down on the edge of a small stream and drank from the cool water and wondered how far he had come and how much further he had to go. He felt terribly lonely.

He struggled slowly through the woods, and came out into the dry, rocky plain, and found a path that led to a small farmhouse he could see in the distance, and wondered if he should go there and ask the way to Balaklava. It occurred to him that he might not be able to make his intentions known to whoever might be there, and it occurred to him, too, that he might find it occupied by the enemy.

There was nothing but silence, broken only by the sounds

of the birds, and he found it strange to ruminate that somewhere in this broken ground a huge force of Russians was searching for what they were sure must be the main body of an equally formidable Allied force.

And then, he heard the sound of galloping horses. There was a moment of panic, and he looked round wildly for somewhere to hide, but it was too late and they were there, in his sight and he in theirs. Then he breathed a sigh of relief for he saw that it was a patrol of Hussars, their colors bright in the sun, their crossbelts gleaming and their brasswork bright and polished, the Army as he had always known it, galloping fast toward him and reining in their horses as they approached. They were led by a sergeant, a tough, thickset man with black hair and beetle-browed eyes just as black.

They were charging hard down on him, and he grinned at them with delight, and then the grin went quickly as he saw the sergeant leveling his lance, and he shouted out:

"No! I'm English!"

They were past him now, the deadly lance pulled back, and they were wheeling their horses to face him again, slowing to a canter and then to a walk. He called out again:

"English! A trooper from the Seventeenth!"

They gathered round him now, and the sergeant reined in his horse, a big mare, sixteen and a half hands or more, and stared down at him for a moment, and said at last, "What's your name, soldier?"

Kirk said smartly: "Alexander Kirkaldy, Sergeant. Seventeenth Lancers."

"And how'd your uniform get into that sorry state, soldier?"

Again, he felt deeply conscious of the dirt and grime. He said lamely, "I've been with the Bashi-Bazouk. They don't seem to hold much with smartness. I was on the field at Alma, and they found me there with a broken leg, smashed by a cannonball.

The shoulder too..." He broke off, wondering about the hard look on the sergeant's face.

The sergeant said, "Alma? That was two weeks ago and more, where have you been since then, soldier?"

"Wandering around, Sergeant. I broke my leg, and a musketball in the shoulder..."

"The Seventeenth weren't at the Alma, you'd better think up a better story, soldier."

"No, the rest of them weren't. But I was." He was conscious that the sergeant wasn't believing a word he said, and he burst out, "For God's sake, I'm an English trooper, don't take me for a Turk!"

"Wandering around. Looking for Russians, no doubt?"

Kirk said proudly, "Yes, Sergeant."

"And who fixed that leg for you?"

The others had not stirred on their horses. They sat on them sternly, bodies erect, waiting for the decision to be made.

Kirk said, "Miss Enderly, she's a nurse, and a sailor name Jack Bates, off the *Arethusa*."

"A sailor? And what's he doing mixing with decent Army folk?"

"Well, he's...he's off one of the ships, the *Arethusa*." Kirk began to realize that perhaps he should have kept quiet about Jack Bates, and he said, "But it was Miss Enderly, really, she fixed me up, her father's one of the merchants."

The sergeant eased himself in the saddle and altered the sit of his belt a trifle. The day was hot, and the jacket was wet with perspiration. He said at last, "You know what we're doing out here, soldier?"

"No, Sergeant, I don't. I don't even know where the army's supposed to be."

"We're out looking for deserters. Does that frighten you any?"

Kirk said steadily, "I'm not a deserter, Sergeant. I'm

THE CHARGE OF THE LIGHT BRIGADE

trying to find my way to a hospital."

"Trying for two weeks, is that it?"

The sergeant eased his great bulk again, cleared his throat and spat, and said, "You know what we do with deserters? We shoot them. But you wouldn't be one of them, would you? Not even after two weeks wandering around, like you call it. Your uniform in rags, with a Turkish dagger in your belt, and the smell of a Turk on you too. What've you really been doing, looting the dead bodies, like the rest of the Turks?"

"No, Sergeant."

"Turn your pockets out. If you've got any pockets left in them rags."

Kirk felt the blood draining from his face unaccountably, and he pulled out the rag that was wrapped around what was left of his meat, and the Sergeant looked at it and said: "Trooper!" and one of the horsemen dismounted, and moved over to Kirk and searched him, and when he held up, silently, the gold medallion for the sergeant to see, Kirk said blustering:

"It belongs to Miss Enderly. She dropped it, you can ask her!"

The sergeant leaned down from the shining saddle, the leather immaculate and rubbed to perfection, and took the gold chain and let it dangle between his fingers, examining it carefully. He said at last, lazily, "Looks just the kind of thing an officer would wear around his neck, don't it? Where did you get it, soldier?"

Kirk said stubbornly: "I told you, Miss Enderly dropped it, and I...I kept it, meaning to give it to her next time we meet."

"...And her father's one of the merchants, yes, I know all about that." He said to the trooper: "Tie him up."

"No! Sergeant! What for?" Kirk's voice held a note of panic.

"What for?" the sergeant echoed mockingly. "What for? I told you, soldier, we shoot deserters. But that's not the half of what we do to them as goes around the battlefields stealing gold medallions off of dead officers. You're coming back with us."

The trooper was patting Kirk's pockets, looking for other items of interest. He took his rifle and knife, and threw away the rag with the meat in it, and then took a piece of leather thong from the pack at his side and bound Kirk's hands behind his back, and found another to tie his ankles tightly together. He pushed him down on the grass, and Kirk said sullenly:

"How am I going to march with you with my feet tied together? I can't hardly walk as it is, not with a busted leg only half mended."

The sergeant said, "You'll stay here, right there where you lie, till we pick you up on the way home."

The trooper spoke for the first time. He said laconically: "Stay with him, Sergeant?"

The sergeant shook his head. "I give you a job to do, to tie him up. You do it proper, he's not going to get away. I need every man of you with me, we got enemy patrols to worry about."

Kirk was furious now. The thongs were biting in his wrists, and the leg was throbbing with the troopers rough handing. He said, scowling, "You got more than patrols to worry about, the whole Russian Army's out here somewhere."

The sergeant said stolidly, "A deserter, and a thief, and a spy as well. And the Russians are not out here, soldier, they're all looked up in Sebastopol, where better men than you are whipping them to their knees."

The trooper was cutting a sapling with this saber, and the sergeant looked around and said, "You'll be seeing your C.O. in a few hour's time, soldier, so you'd better start praying."

The trooper stuck the sapling in the ground, close by him and tied a rag to its top, marking the spot, and said with satisfaction, "That's five of them now, not a bad day's work."

"Mount up, trooper, and keep your trap shut." The

THE CHARGE OF THE LIGHT BRIGADE

Sergeant wheeled his horse and sank in his spurs. The mare plunged forward, the dust flying under her hooves, and the others followed. They did not look back once, and soon the sound of them had gone; only the dust hung heavy in the air to mark their passing.

For a short while, a few short minutes, Kirk lay there, still and silent and furious. And then, painfully, he began to roll himself over to the stream where he had been drinking before. He worked his body around in the pebbles at the water's edge till his hands, tightly bound behind his back, were deep under the water. He waited a while till the leather was soft, and then began to work his wrists, favoring his right arm and saving the effort of his left where the pain was.

Soon he could feel the thong stretching, and he strained at it mightily till it was loose enough to work his hands around freely. And, in a little under half an hour, his hands were free again. He untied the bindings around his ankles, moved back and found his crutch, and his knife, and his rifle, and hurried as best he could in the direction the patrol had come from.

He saw the white rag on the sapling soon; and there, in the grass beside it, bound just as he had been, was a trooper from the Inniskillings. He bent down and cut the thongs and said roughly:

"All right, you're on your own, they'll be back within the hour."

The trooper looked at him, puzzled. His sharp, ferret eyes took in the frayed blue jacket and the scarred leather, and he said: "Lancers? Come with me, chum. I know where there's money to be had for the taking."

Kirk frowned. "Money?"

"Yes, four dead officers, a major and three lieutenants. They caught me when I'd just started going through their pockets, and tell you..." He broke off, then said eagerly, "You found a hatter way to live in this heathen land?"

Kirk said again, "You're on your own. Go back and find the others, there are three more back there somewhere. Cut them free and be on your way." He turned and moved off, not looking back. He was conscious that the cruel, ignorant eyes were still on him.

Soon he was finding his way back to the mountain, keeping to the woods, away from the road, his eyes and his ears alert, and watching anxiously for the sergeant and his men. He crossed through the copse and down into the little valley, and up the other side again, and when the evening came he was sure that at last he had eluded any possible pursuit.

He could not know it, but less than an hour after leaving him there, like a trussed turkey, the sergeant and his men had blundered into the Russian vanguard; all of them had been killed in the first exchange of shots.

He climbed in the darkness to the top of the mountain, and there was Bates, dozing by the light of the fire among the rocks, and he flopped down heavily beside him, and touched his hand. Close by Epernon opened his eyes and shut them again, and Bates said softly, "Glad you made it back, boy. Now, get some sleep, we'll talk in the morning."

It was good to be with his friends again. Kirk closed his exhausted eyes and slept like a child.

CHAPTER 7

In the early morning, Bates said nothing of Kirk's attempt to leave them. He was cautious, reserved, and a trifle distant, as though wondering whether the boy's return were really a case of taking the second best, but the mood soon passed.

One of the scouts came in and held a long discourse with Mahmoud, and Mahmoud listened carefully, and looked around at the high mountains and the deep-scarred plains, with the gorges and the valleys running through them like jagged slices in the hard earth, and he blew his nose noisily with his fingers, and said to Bates:

"We must move east, my friend." He pointed to the east and said, "There, in the valleys, the Russians are beginning to move. They move on Balaklava."

"At last. And for once, it makes sense. If they take Balaklava away from us, the whole British Army's cut off."

Even the bumbling General Menshikov had stumbled on the obvious. The assault force of the Allies was ringed around Sebastopol, on the uplands, its rear protected by the tenuous line of the Ninety-third's five hundred Highlanders, a thousand Turks, and a single field battery under Colonel Maude. And against them, Menshikov was readying twenty-five battalions of his infantry and thirty-four squadrons of cavalry, a total of more than twenty-four thousand men, backed up with seventy-eight guns. The patrolling days and nights were over; now the assault was to begin.

Mahmoud said dryly, "And better we move, they come this way."

Bates sighed. "Any good sending to tell them again that their rear's being threatened?"

Mahmoud shrugged: "I send three men to the Nizam, only the Turks will listen to us. I tell them to tell your commander too, but..." He spat his contempt.

In the Allied lines, the use of information from spies was frowned upon and regarded always with a great deal of distrust. In a gentleman's war, should the views of a spy, and a heathen spy at that, be countenanced?

The Nizam to whom Mahmoud's men had reported during the night were camped on the Causeway heights, and they had sent word of the impending Russian attack to Sir Colin Campbell, commander of the Highland Brigade. Campbell had informed Lord Raglan, who had pondered the advisability of verifying this alarming but, no doubt, untrustworthy news, and had finally sent Sir George Catheart with eight hundred men of his Fourth Division to scour the heights in a nighttime search. The men had spent the rest of the night uselessly scouring the hills, shivering in the Crimean cold which soon, with the advent of winter, was to kill so many thousands of them, and had reported back to his commander in chief that the report was false.

Epernon said, delighting in his appraisal of his late comrades, "What is the use of telling them, my friend? They will not believe what they do not see with their own eyes. They believe that the Russians are as foolish as they are themselves."

Bates said, "Tell the men to ride out. There's not enough of us left to do much, but...with a few quick assaults on their flanks as they move in formation, we can at least harass them and maybe start them firing too soon. If we can get them to open up with the heavy gun on us..."

Mahmoud yelled an order to the men, and they began stamping out the fires and mounting up, yelling insults and boasts at each other.

Kirk was binding a new rag round the lower part of his leg, and he came over to them and asked, "Are we moving? This is a good place for us to be, Jack..."

Bates told him: "The Russkies are getting their army together, they'll be moving this way. And we're too exposed here. We're moving down to the valley where the broken ground is, down by that place they call the Valley of the Shadow of Death." (This valley was one of two that cut deep into the hills from the inlet that formed Sebastopol harbor, the other was called the Great Ravine. But neither of these two valleys was the one that was to be immortalized later as the scene of the Light Brigades famous charge, which was not truly a valley at all but merely an opening between two hills.) Bates went on, "From there, we can keep an eye to the south, and if the Russkies break out of Sebastopol we'll know that too..."

He broke off, startled by the look on Kirk's face. He said, "What is it, boy?"

Kirk said quickly, "Jenny. She's over at the Tulan farmhouse, camped there with one man to look after her."

"Then we'd better get her out of there, quickly. Wait here with Frenchy." He turned away, but Kirk stopped him and said, "I'll come with you, Jack."

"I'm riding, Kirk. There's not much time."

"Then I'll ride too."

"With a busted leg? You're not ready yet for a horse."

"I'm a better rider with one leg than any sailor is with two, even a sailor from the *Arethusa*."

And Epernon laughed and backed him up, "Let him go too, Jacques. Sooner or later he will have to ride again, and to see his girl..."

Bates shrugged. "If you can face it, Kirk..."

They went over together to where their horses were, and Bates carefully selected a small pony, no more than twelve and a half hands high, and helped Kirk into the saddle, and Kirk said, his face drawn with sudden pain:

"Tie the leg, Jack, tie it down to the bellyband."

"And if your horse stumbles and falls?"

"With me on his back he won't stumble. A good little horse and a good little rider too. Tie it. Not too tight."

Bates took a soft rope of camel's hair and bound the ankle firmly to the wide embroidered strap, and he looked up at Kirk's white face and said, "Yell if you want to, Kirk..."

Kirk shook his head, his lips tight. He was breathing heavily, sucking in his cheeks, and he pulled on the single rein and swung the horse round and began to walk him. As Bates mounted up and followed, Kirk spurred the pony into a canter and then into a gallop, and Bates moved fast to overtake him, hanging on tight to the high pommel till they moved out onto easier ground. He caught up at last and saw the boy's white face, and as they galloped side by side, he called out: "We can walk the horses..."

Kirk shook his head and laughed suddenly and called back, "It's fine, Jack, its fine! It's good to be in the saddle again!"

The pain was excruciating, and he gritted his teeth and galloped on, bearing tight with his good leg and feeling the strain of the binding rope on the other. The blood was pounding in it, and even the bones were throbbing.

They moved down the steep hill at the gallop, and increased their pace when they came to the dirt road at the bottom, riding fast for the trees that would give them cover here in no-man's land, forcing the horses and themselves to the utmost of endurance. They crashed into the trees, sweeping under

THE CHARGE OF THE LIGHT BRIGADE

low-hanging branches, bending low over their horses' necks as they forced a way through the undergrowth.

They rode for fifteen minutes, slowed to a walk now, and suddenly Bates called urgently, "Cover!"

They swung their mounts round and headed deeper into the undergrowth, crashing through the saplings that bent under the impact of their momentum. And when they pulled up at last, Bates saw that Kirk was swaying in his saddle, his eyes wide and his face white as a sheet, and he dismounted quickly and went over to him, and pulled his knife and cut the binding round the ankle, and caught the boy as he fell from the saddle and dragged him quickly away, paying no attention to the blood on his lip. And when at last they were far from the horses, he laid him down on the nettles there and put a hand over his mouth and whispered, "No sound, Kirk."

Kirk's eyes were wide, but he looked up and nodded, and Bates took his hand away quietly and began to load his rifle, pushing the long ramrod home and peering out through the bushes.

They heard them now, the rushing sound of a body of horsemen. And soon, on the narrow track that ran close by, they saw a patrol of forty or fifty men ride by at a gallop, tall Cossacks in long gray coats, moving fast in spite of the difficulty of the terrain, their lances held high and their sabers clattering against the metalwork of their saddles. They saw the officer at their head slice through an overhanging branch with his sword as he galloped.

And then, they were gone, and there was silence again.

They waited a long time, the two of them, crouched under the bushes and listening. And at last Kirk said, his voice a whisper, "They've come from Tulan's farm..."

Bates nodded, his face set. "Aye, maybe they have."

Kirk was dragging himself painfully to his feet, stumbling off toward the horses, his bad leg dragging.

Bates followed him urgently. "Your leg, can you still ride?"

"I'll manage. She's maybe in a worse state than I am. Come on, give me a leg up, and leave the ankle untied, I've a mind to learn to use it."

They mounted up again, and Bates said, "Haste or no, Kirk, we'll walk the horses now. There's maybe more of them around."

"We'll gallop."

They rode fast, back to the track and along it, the dust of the Russians still heavy in the dry air. And when they came to the clearing where the small field was already knee-high in neglected weeds, they took cover, and stood for a long while at the edge of the trees, watching and waiting and listening.

The dogcart was there, its long shafts high in the air, and the dog lay dead on the ground near the stone wall of the well, of Jenny, there was no sign.

Bates whispered; "Stay here, Kirk, keep mounted. At the first sign of trouble, ride out."

"I'll stay and back you up." Kirk began to load his rifle, moving his horse deeper under cover and taking the loose rein of Bates' mount. Bates moved off silently, his body low to the ground, snaking his way through the weeds toward the tiny house.

Kirk watched him go, and then he raised his rifle at a movement in the door of the barn, and Jenny Enderly was there, running out from the barn toward the dead dog, dropping to her knees beside it. Kirk spurred his horse and galloped forward, shouting to Bates as he went. He saw Bates rise up like a ghost out of the grass and come running towards them, and then he was pulling up close beside Jenny and shouting, "We must leave here now, quickly."

Jenny looked up at him, then down at the dog, and said, "Why did they have to kill him...?"

THE CHARGE OF THE LIGHT BRIGADE

Kirk slipped painfully from the saddle, twisting his body round and lowering himself gently to the ground with a strong hold on the pommel. He turned to her and took her by the shoulders and said, "Are you all right? Did you see them? What happened?"

Jenny said, "The dog barked, and I went to the barn and let him loose, and he ran out and...yes, I saw them, a long column of them come riding in, riding hard, and they killed the dog and two of them went into the house..."

"And your bodyguard?"

Bates was coming up to them now, and he said urgently, "We can't stand here in the open, there may be more of them."

Jenny turned to the barn, and the peasant was there, stumbling out, his rifle at the ready, and she turned back and said, "He wanted to fire at them, but I wouldn't let him."

Bates said grimly, "You were right. More than fifty or sixty of them, you'd better come with us."

"No. I must get to Balaklava."

Kirk said, holding her still, speaking very gently: "Come with us, Jenny, you'll be safer. They're mounting an attack on Balaklava, the whole Russian Army's moving in."

She stared, "No, it can't be! I was at Lord Raglan's camp this morning, he told me himself, all the Russians are locked up in Sebastopol."

Dismayed, Kirk stared at Bates, "Then they still don't believe us."

Jenny said, insisting: "The Highlanders are holding this area, the Ninety-third."

"And the Russians are all around them, on the heights and in the valleys, too."

Not believing, she asked: "Then who's defending Sebastopol?"

"More of them. Fifty thousand of them, maybe. Doesn't Raglan understand that?"

"I don't know..." Then she said, hesitantly: "There've been patrols out there all night, they saw nothing."

Kirk said bitterly, "The whole country's thick with them, and nobody knows where they are."

Bates interrupted them: "Never mind about that, let's get away from here. This place smells of trouble. We've two horses, we'll get you back to our camp, your man too."

He was standing there silently, the peasant, a short, stubby man with dark face and black intelligent eyes.

Jenny said impatiently: "To your camp? With the Bashi-Bazouk? He's a Greek, my man, and you know what the Turks think of the Greeks, they'd kill him just for the joy of it. And I won't go there either. If what you say is true, I'll be needed in Balaklava soon. I'll thank you for your help, but I'll take the track to the harbor, it's only a mile or two."

Bates said again, his voice impatient: "Lets get to the woods, we can't stand here and argue all day. Come on..." He was already moving back toward the copse, away from the open field, urging them to follow him.

They went with him, their rifles at the ready, their eyes searching for any sign of more danger. As they hurried, Jenny took Kirk's arm to help him, but he pulled himself away from her and said roughly, "I can manage."

She looked at him, seeing how he tried to hide the limp, and said, "Is it healing slowly, is it getting strong again?" He nodded.

Behind them, Bates said caustically, "And now he's riding already. He's going to be a cripple for life."

They ploughed their way through the long grass, with anxious glances from side to side. Bates gave his horse to Jenny and helped Kirk to mount up, tying the ankle once more to the bellystrap, and walked beside them slowly, the Greek walking ahead of them and searching the bushes with his sharp eyes as he went, walking in silence and not looking back at them.

THE CHARGE OF THE LIGHT BRIGADE

They spoke quietly. Jenny said somberly; "I think this war will never be over. And if the truth were known, it should never have started."

Kirk was ill at ease, knowing that there was a gap between them that could not properly be bridged, a gap that was the emptiness of his education. He said, moving out of his depth, "The Russians, they've always caused us trouble, even when we were fighting the French."

"It's that Navy of theirs," Bates said darkly. "We've got to keep their ships out of the Mediterranean, it's an English lake."

For ninety years the major powers had been squabbling over the use of the Dardanelles and the Bosporus. The Black Sea and the Straits had long since been opened, by the Treaty of Kuchuk Kainarji in 1774, to Russian vessels in times of peace, but this was not good enough for the Czar, who wanted free access in times of war as well. But the fear of armed Russian vessels in the Mediterranean had always been a nightmare for the Western Powers, a contingency toward which every French and British diplomatic endeavor had always been aimed; and the true purpose of this war, even though its ostensible cause was the spluttering fuse of the trifling trouble in the Holy Land, was the urgent need of the Allies to deny the Dardanelles to the expansive imperial ambitions of the Czar Nicholas, like Peter the Great, like Boris Godunov and Ivan the Terrible, like all the rulers of the Tartary hordes before him, had long dreamed of expansion to the south and the east.

Bates said again, in the silence, doggedly, "We've got to keep them out of the Mediterranean, or England's lost."

Jenny looked down at him, wondering about the stubborn determination of a man who had deserted his fleet. She said, challenging him, "Just what are you doing here, Bates?"

It seemed she had forgotten, or had not known, that they had come to help her. He looked at her in surprise.

"Here, Ma'am? We came down to take you away from Tulan's farm, soon as we heard the Russkies were gathering."

"No, before that? You deserted your ship, and yet...yet you're still fighting. You're fighting among savages instead of with your own people."

"And I don't tip my hat to nobody now, Ma'am. Does that answer your question?"

They pushed their way through the rustling foliage, and Bates said, pressing his argument, "I was a good sailor, a master gunner, maybe the best in the Fleet, and I seen the way we was fighting this war. Not to win it, Ma'am, just to fight it. You know what I mean? If we'd fought this war the way it should have been fought, the way the Duke of Wellington would have fought it, it'd be over and done with now, and I'd be home with my family instead of wandering around a foreign country with a bunch of savages, as you call them. But we didn't, and it's not over, and maybe it'll go on forever. And what will it have done when it's all over? I'll tell you what, Ma'am, nothing! I didn't desert because I'm against the war, I deserted because I'm against the way they're fighting it. Young Kirk now, for him, it's different. He cleared out because he's sick of the fighting, only he can't make up his mind what to do next. He's only a boy, and that's understandable, because at his age a man can see what's wrong and still not know what to do about it. But for me, in my humble way I'm doing what *they* should be doing: I'm fighting the Russkies and I'm doing it better than I ever did before. I'm an old man now, Ma'am, and I know where I'm going."

Kirk said angrily, "And I don't?"

"Do you, boy?"

Kirk bit his lip and looked at Jenny. He said: "Yes, I'm sick of the fighting and I don't care who knows it. We'll win this war; sooner or later. I'm sure of that. We *always* win our wars, everyone knows that. The British Army has never been defeated yet. But if a man's got to die, it's fitting that he should die at home, among his own people, and know what he's dying for, not bleeding to death, neglected, in a foreign land and not knowing the reason why. Not trying to answer questions he doesn't even understand. All right, what the Russians are up to is no good, I knew that, but we're a civilized nation and when we don't agree with a man we ought to be able to find a better way to convince him than killing off all our own young men trying to change his mind." He said moodily, "They burned a man, alive..."

He saw Jenny looking at him strangely and he said, half angrily, "I've come to my senses, and because of it, I'll never see my home again, maybe. I don't like to think about it."

Bates said gently, "Your home's here now, Kirk. Back home, they'll shoot you. A deserter, just like me. Just like Frenchy. We've made up our minds about it, and you'd better do the same. We'll stay here till the war's won, and then...then there'll be other wars fight, and there's always a place for a man who can use a gun and live by his wits."

Kirk's sudden anger had gone. He said dryly, "The prospect ahead of us; it's not much of a life, Jack, is it?"

"You want to join the thin red line again, is that it? You want to stand there while they bowl red-hot cannonballs at you, stand there with your officer checking your dressing and the shine of your leather while your friends are dropping all around you and lying there till they die? Is that what you want?"

Kirk said quietly, "No, Jack, I just want no more part of it. No more killing."

The bright greens of the hazel woods opened up into a clearing, and there was a thick stand of hawthorn, with wild blackberries growing and bees humming about them. They reined in the horses and stood for a while looking out on the plain that lay before them.

The white bell tents of the Highlanders were there, with

the hills rising on all sides of them and narrow, sandy roads crisscrossing the plain. There were packhorses, heavily laden, champing at the grass, and a score of fires were sending up spirals of blue smoke into the still air. On a small hillock they could see the guns of Colonel Maude's battery. A rider was cantering down from them toward the officers' tents where the regimental colors were flying. The plain, a mile or two across, was dominated on all sides by the hills, red sandstone hills cut deeply by narrow gorges and spread with deep-green carpets of grass and great patches of yellow broom. The nearest tents were no more than a thousand yards away.

They sat their horses and watched for a moment, and Kirk said miserably, "There's a thousand Turks down there somewhere, and not a sign of nary a one of them, because it makes sense to keep out of sight when the enemy's all around you. But the Highlanders...look at them! The colors flying and the mules staked out and a hundred tents in full view. They could ride down from the hills, the Cossacks, and cut them to pieces before they could ever sound the Stand-to."

Through the dip in the hills they could see a white mud building, roofed in red tile, with a rickety fence around it and some pigs wallowing in the mud there. Beyond it they could just make out the furled topsails and the rigging of a man of war in the harbor.

Jenny slid down from her horse and said urgently, "Come with me, Kirk. Come to Balaklava with me. It's not too late."

He shook his head stubbornly, "It's not possible, Jenny." He wanted to tell her about the sergeant, about his brush with the patrol the previous day. But he could not bring himself to tell her of the contempt his own troops now had for him. He said hesitantly and not even sure that he was telling the truth, "My place is here now, Jenny, a new sort of life I'll have to learn about."

"For how long, Kirk? For how *long?*"

THE CHARGE OF THE LIGHT BRIGADE

He shook his head. "I don't know, and that's a fact. But, as long as maybe. Tomorrow might be different, or the day after, or the day after that. Who knows what there is ahead of me now? But whatever there is waiting for me, I'll have to face it. And that's what I'll do, Jenny, face it."

Bates said urgently, "We'd better get away from here, Kirk. Look there."

Kirk turned. Eight hundred yards down the slope, a lieutenant, his body ramrod staff, his leatherwork shining, the tall bearskin heavy and solid above the bright red coat, was cantering toward them.

Jenny said quickly, "Then, go now." She turned away and began to move down the hill toward the officer and the tents as the Greek plodded silently beside her.

Kirk eased himself in the saddle, holding on with both hands, and turned away to press the horse back among the trees. He was aware that Bates was following, but he did not look back.

And soon, the camp was hidden behind them, masked by the soft greens of the trees as they rode fast through the forest, back to the safety of their hidden camp in no-man's land.

CHAPTER 8

Back at the camp, he could not get the thought of Jenny out of his mind. He said angrily, "What's she doing, wandering all over the plain like that? They shouldn't let her."

Bates grimaced. "A stubborn woman, you can see that by the set of her mouth. And she has a job to do, Kirk, a job she wished upon herself. We could have done with a few like her on the *Arethusa*."

"When women come to the aid of the soldiers," Epernon said carefully, "do you know what this means? It means that the consciousness of war is seeping down from the army to the civilians. And the logical progression is this, that one day, when there is a war, everybody will be involved in it."

"Civilians too?" Bates asked scornfully. "You talk a lot of rubbish, Frenchy."

"Perhaps. But when nurses want to leave the base and follow the men into the field, this, my friend, is the first step toward the perdition of all fighting men like you and me."

"A nurse's' place is back at the base, with the hospitals, not in the field. And yet..." Wondering about it, Kirk said, "All they see fit to give us on the field is a few old pensioners who are good for nothing but carrying stretchers, if they ever have any stretchers. There was a boy close beside me at the Alma, we crossed the river together, at arm's length, a boy younger than me, not much more than fifteen, maybe sixteen, years old. He fell before we'd reached a hundred yards above the bank, a bullet through the knee, that's all it was. Just a musket ball. He was beside me while we lay in the grass, for an hour and a half, and he didn't make a sound, and when they told us to get up and start advancing again, I called to him and waited. But I couldn't lose my dressing, because my lieutenant was there, right in front of me, and when I looked back, the boy was dead. His name was Johnny, not much more than fifteen years old. A bullet in the knee, that's all it was, and if we'd had someone like Jenny there...who knows, she might have been able to save him."

"You'll have the women up there with the troops, is that what you want?" Bates said sardonically, "There are better places for a good woman to be. Back home with her family, that's where she belongs. In bed, in the kitchen...the field of battle's no place for a woman. And, aye, you're right, they've no call to be letting her wander around like that, the wounded should take their chances like the rest of us."

Bates was staring down the slope. In the evening light, Mahmoud was climbing up toward them, his stride long and slow. He was carrying his beads in both hands, moving them gently along the string, counting his sins. He came up and squatted down beside them, and looked up at the sky and said, "A fine day tomorrow."

He lifted a stone and spat carefully under it and as carefully replaced it. He grinned and said, "A beautiful woman, the Ingles woman who make the boy's leg better."

Kirk looked at him, puzzled and Bates said softly, "What's on your mind, heathen?"

"A beautiful woman will make a fine wife one day, maybe." He tucked his long robe around his legs and squatted there, staring at the ground, his knees up under his chin, his heels flat on the ground.

Epernon looked at Bates and said quietly, "I think we have trouble here." He turned to Mahmoud and said, "We are waiting, friend."

Mahmoud sighed. It was not good to come to the business in hand so abruptly. He spat again and looked up at the sky and said, "I think maybe we do not see her again."

Kirk reached out and grabbed him by the cloth under his chin and said savagely, "What is it you have to say about her, Mahmoud? Tell me or, by God..."

Epernon put out a hand and restrained him and said, his eyes bright and alert, "No, Kirk, in good time, in his own good time."

Mahmoud took Kirk's wrist in a steel grip and twisted the arm round and sent him sprawling on the ground and, not changing his position, he looked at him with his black eyes alive with mischief. He said, "I tell you, woman. The other woman is with the Russians now, your Ingles woman."

Kirk lay on the ground and stared, and Bates got quickly to his feet and helped him up and turned to Mahmoud and said urgently, "Tell me, Mahmoud." His voice was cold and authoritative, and Epernon nodded and said gently, "We are your friends, you must tell us."

Mahmoud spat under the stone again and laughed suddenly and put out a helping hand to Kirk. He said, "Over to the north, a Russian patrol, one of many Russian patrols... They find the Ingles woman riding along the Woronzoff road to look for wounded men." He shrugged. "Wounded men, better she should let them die and go to their gods."

Bates said steadily, "And where is she now?"

Mahmoud shrugged, "One of their patrols, fifteen, twenty men, all Cossacks. One of my scouts come in and tell me, they find her. They kill the Greek who is with her because he is a Greek, it is good." He grinned and drew a finger across his neck

THE CHARGE OF THE LIGHT BRIGADE

and said, "They cut off the Greek's head, it is good."

Kirk's face was white, "And Jenny? Miss...Miss Enderly?"

Mahmoud shrugged again; he was not too concerned over the fate of a woman, even though she was close to these friends of his. He said, "My scout tell me that they will take her back to their camp. He tell me that the Russians say she is spy for Ingles."

Kirk, white-faced, was on his feet again, his stick neglected. He said urgently, "Will you come with me, Jack?"

Epernon said; "Wait, we all go." He turned to Mahmoud and said, "Fifteen men? Twenty? Or how many?"

Mahmoud shrugged. "Maybe fifty."

"Cossacks? All of them?"

"Cossacks."

"Headed where?"

"They go to their camp on Kamara Hill."

"Which way?"

"They pass to the north of the hill that you call Canrobert. There is a deep *wadi* there, where the red rocks are."

"I know it."

Bates said; "Are you with us?"

Mahmoud raised his shoulders, "If we fight, I am with you. Am I too a woman that I should not fight?"

Kirk had found his horse and was pulling himself up into the saddle, biting his lip against the pain, Mahmoud shouted, and the Bashi-Bazouk were mounting their ponies, swinging themselves lightly into the saddles and letting the horses prance and churn up the dust while they waited for their leader.

The men gathered together in a little group and Bates said calmly; "We ride due south and cut them off where the *wadi* breaks out into the woods, where it hits the Causeway. There's cover among the trees there. Mahmoud and three men take the north side of the *wadi* and Suleiman... Can Suleiman ride again?"

Mahmoud jeered. "My cousin, a strong man, he can ride better than any one of us, and fight better too, Ingles."

"Then Suleiman and the rest of us to the south of it, except for Epernon and Kirk." He turned to Kirk. "You and Frenchy ride in behind them, to turn them round, and as soon as they hit you we'll come in on the flanks, understood?"

Kirk shouted, "Understood, let's ride!"

He had already turned his horse and was urging it down the slope. He was riding better now, dispensing with the rope that once had tied his wounded leg into place. Epernon and Bates were close behind, and soon the rest of them, with Mahmoud at their head, were cutting off at a tangent, instinctively searching for better ground where their sure-footed ponies could gallop the faster. In a loose, untidy column, their rifles held high and their shouts filling the air, they were racing across the sand and the grass, the dust flying up under the horses' hooves as they hurtled down the hill to the *wadi* that led into the copse of beeches and ash and poplar.

The darkness was deep and impenetrable, and there was only the sound of them to show where they were going.

The horses stood miraculously quiet in two little groups, one on either side of the deep water, where tiny rivulets carved their way in the soft red earth. It was as though they had been trained to a silence as close as that of the riders, who sat astride them, with their rifles cradled, motionless and menacing in the light of the moon. Even the night birds were silent.

They were below the ridge in the darkness, each of the two groups, four men on one side and three on the other, dappled with the light of the moon that streamed once in a while through the clouds and the shaded foliage of the dark trees. And above them, the end of the gully, Mahmoud and Suleiman el Kebir, the giant, lay silent on their bellies, listening to the sounds of the distant Cossacks as they came, riding slowly at the walk, down the trail. Their bodies, dressed in soil-dirty rags, were part of the

THE CHARGE OF THE LIGHT BRIGADE

earth itself; only their eyes were moving. Suleiman reached out and spun a small stone across the gorge, and on the other side Mahmoud crept away, his body slithering down to where Bates sat his horse, silent and still, with two of the Bashi-Bazouk close beside him, their draw swords glistening in the pale glow of the night.

His voice was a whisper. "Now, Ingles, in one minute or two..."

Bates nodded. They waited. The clouds moved across the moon, and the darkness was there again, and Mahmoud's white teeth gleamed brightly. He grinned and whispered, "You see? Even Allah is on our side tonight."

Then, it came, the sound they had been waiting for. There was a single shot from a musket and the sudden sound of galloping hooves. They could hear two horses moving fast, racing down on the patrol from the rear, and they heard Epernon's wild, excited yells. They heard a shout in Russian, heard the whole patrol, now no more than a hundred feet away from them, wheeling round to face the surprise attack, wheeling to face an unknown threat from the rear.

Bates shouted out loudly, "Now!" and spurred his horse forward, up the slope and with a leap down into the *wadi*. Not waiting for the others, knowing they were close beside him, he raced toward the enemy horsemen, no more than a blurred nebulous mass in the darkness. He fired his musket into them, then threw it down and raised his sword, the old Navy cutlass he treasured so dearly, and slashed at the first body that came across his path, feeling the keen edge cut through the heavy overcoat and into yielding flesh.

He saw Epernon forcing his horse deep among them, slashing with his saber in a kind of furious abandon, his white teeth gleaming in his dark face, moving with incredible speed in and out again, his horse rearing as he cut and parried, sliced and lunged. He was fighting like a madman, with no thought other than to kill, to carve a way deep into the tightly pressed horsemen who were all around him.

A Cossack to one sides of Bates raised his lance to drive it through his body with a downward stroke, and as Bates turned he saw the tip of Epernon's sword go through the man's throat, and Epernon laughed and yelled his delight.

The clouds moved past the moon, and in the moment of brightness Bates saw Suleiman riding in on the other flank with his men, four of them close behind him. He saw the Russians wheel to face him, their tight-packed horses rearing up and kicking out with their forelegs. He saw the little cart in an opening they had made, and he spurred his horse toward it, cutting and slicing with his weapon, feeling the edge of a lance slice at his leg as he cut at the shoulders of the man who was wielding it, seeing him topple off his horse and fall under its belly.

He threw himself out of the saddle and into the cart, falling over its wooden rails with the impetus of the movement and knowing instinctively that the horse beside him now was Kirk's, and that Kirk was reaching out with straining arms. Bates lay on his back there for a moment, the wind knocked out of him, and then he found his feet and grabbed the thin frail form that seemed lifeless and stood with it on the cart's sloping floor, stumbling against its side. Then he threw her body across Kirk's saddle and yelled, "Ride!"

He found the cutlass he had dropped and slashed at the face of a horseman who was raising his sword high above his head, heard his scream as the steel bit into bone. And then, Mahmoud was there, forcing himself through the throng, bringing up the horse, and he was in the saddle again and urging the animal forward, while close beside him he could see the hulk of the giant Suleiman, using two swords and clearing a path for him.

And then, suddenly, in the confusion, they were all clear

and moving fast up the slope of the gully, wheeling round to ride along its top for half a mile at the gallop, then down into it again and up the other side and away toward the woods.

He was aware, Bates, that there was a single horseman ahead of him now, and he spurred his mount on and caught up, and saw Kirk three, with Jenny across his saddle, riding hard and looking back at him and grinning. And when they reached the woods, they slipped off their horses and waited among the bushes, and soon Mahmoud and his men came up and reined in hard, the horses sending up clouds of dust as they pranced.

They swung round to face any possible pursuit, and waited in silence, and at last Mahmoud said, "Nothing. They will not follow us here."

Bates looked around at the men in the darkness. He said, "Where's Suleiman?"

Kirk shook his head. "I saw him a few moments ago, he was close behind me. Did they follow us?"

"Only along the gully, I lost them then."

They waited a while, and then Bates said grimly, "Wait for me here." He rode out, cantering in the darkness.

Kirk bent over Jenny's prostrate form. Her wrists had been tied behind her back, cruelly tight, and he took his knife and cut the ropes, and he poured water from his canteen between her pale lips while Mahmoud and the others stood by and stared down at them, looking off among the trees at the sound of every snapping twig or softly rustling lizard.

He whispered, "Jenny, are you all right? It's me, Kirk..."

She opened her eyes then and stared up at him in horror, and he brushed the blood from his face, the blood where a saber had taken him across the cheek, and he said, "It's nothing, are you hurt? Are you hurt badly?"

She shook her head. "Oh, Kirk..." She shook her head from side to side, her eyes filled with tears, and said. "The Greek, they killed him. They tied his hands behind his back and they cut off his head."

"Yes, yes, I know. It's all over now, you're going to be all right."

She buried her face in her hands and began to sob, and Mahmood said roughly, "Quiet!"

A horseman was moving in, and soon Bates was there. He slipped down quickly from the saddle and looked at Jenny and said, "Is she going to be all right?"

Kirk nodded. "And Suleiman?"

There was a moment of silence. Bates said, "Dead. Out there on the grass with a Cossack lance between his shoulder blades." He looked at Mahmoud and said, "A good man, Mahmoud, I'm sorry he's gone."

Mahmoud's eyes flickered. His face was grim, but he shrugged and said softly, "It is good for a strong man to die in battle. Should he die of old age, or hunger, or disease? No, it is better so." He turned away and began to count his beads.

"Why didn't they follow us?" Kirk asked. "They must have known we were only a handful."

He heard Mahmoud grunt, and Bates said, "They've been hit by the Bashi-Bazouk before. They suspected a trap, they thought we might be trying to draw them into an ambush. They learn their lessons fast, the Russkies. No, they won't follow us now. We took their captive, and they'll go back to their camp and say that they killed her when she tried to escape."

Jenny was rubbing at her chafed wrists, sitting on the ground with her long white dress torn and mud-died, and Bates said, "And now, Ma'am? What now?"

She looked up at him: "Now?"

"Where shall we take you, Ma'am? It's a long way to Balaklava, and the ground's thick with their patrols, so maybe you'd better get up on the Sapoune Ridge where the other ladies are camped? The whole army's up there somewhere, and right in the middle of them's about the only safe place to be just now.

THE CHARGE OF THE LIGHT BRIGADE

We can get you within sight of their tents, maybe, in a few hours, if we don't run into any more trouble. But you'd be better off staying with us."

She said somberly, "A man was killed, what was his name? Suleiman?"

"They called him 'El Kebir', the giant," Kirk said. "A good man, one of the best."

"And for me..."

"They would have shot you, as a spy, did you know that?"

"Yes. Yes, they told me. They laughed about it." She flared suddenly and said, "A spy! I was bringing in two wounded men, trying to get them back to the camp." She began to cry again and said. "They killed them too, two badly wounded men, they ran their lances though them. What kind of savages are they?"

Bates said stolidly, "We're all savages. Ma'am, when it comes to fighting a war, and it doesn't matter how or when a man is killed if he's the enemy. Which is what those two men were for the Russians. Mercy's a fine and chivalrous thing when a battles starting out, but when the fighting's been going on for a while, a man gets...calloused. Yes, he becomes a savage, if you like, and it's savages, not gentlemen, who win wars."

"But you don't kill the wounded..."

"Maybe it's more merciful at that."

"No. They had hope for life, both of them. And now..."

Mahmoud said quietly, "Better we leave this place. I do not like it here."

It was an instinct the Bashi-Bazouk had developed. Cut off from the main forces of their own people, operating in stealth and darkness in the hills that could be empty of life one moment and alive with the enemy the next, that instinct was all a man had, sometimes, to save his own neck, and it was never questioned.

Jenny found a clean piece of her dress and tore it off, and bound it round Kirk's face where the saber had sliced deep into the bone. She said: "When we get to Sapoune Ridge I'll see that you get proper treatment."

He shook his head. "No, Jenny, we'll leave you within sight of the camp, we won't go into it. I'm a deserter, and they know that now."

This time, she did not argue. She shook her head miserably and said. "All right, if that's what you think is best."

They mounted their horse, Jenny riding with Bates, and when he turned and started to move west, toward the uplands, Mahmoud said roughly, "No, to the north, we cannot ride in the valley now."

Bates turned. "Why not?"

Mahmoud spat. "The Russians were riding with their swords in their sheaths, and they were making noise, did you not hear them talking? It means that, for them, this is no longer a dangerous place because there are others of them nearby. And that means that, for us... No, we must ride away from here to the east, and if we go to the ridge, then we must do this in daylight, when we can see them and run fast if we have to. With an Ingles woman in our midst, how can we fight? You see? She makes cowards even of the Bashi-Bazouk. We should have let the Russians keep her."

Bates was worried. The Allies, and safety, lay to the west. He said stubbornly; "If there are patrols, we'll slip through them in the dark, we've done it before."

Mahmoud gestured at the sky. "The moon, it is too bright."

Kirk said, "It's likely they're in force in the valley tonight. If they're mounting an attack on Balaklava, they'll be scouting out the lie of the land in the darkness. Mahmoud's right. By daylight, they'll be back in the hills again or on the other side of the Causeway, up above the north valley. In daylight, we can ride in the lee of the Woronzoff road clear up to the ridge."

Bates hesitated. "And if our own troops see us?"

"Then we leave Jenny to them and ride out. They won't follow us, we're Bashi-Bazouk."

"All right." Bates swung his horse round. The little party moved off to the east, walking their horses in the silence and the darkness.

As Mahmoud eased his mount in close beside him, Kirk said quietly, "If there's any trouble, Mahmoud, we run. We don't stand and fight, we run. Is that understood?"

Mahmoud grinned. "One time in my life I will run. All right, Ingles, we keep your woman safe for you."

They ran twice during the few remaining hours of darkness.

Once, while easing along the southern lee of the ridge, they stumbled into a long line of horsemen who were moving southwest toward Kadikoi, and they turned aside and galloped fast to the north to avoid them. And when they reached the Causeway and began to cross it, cautiously now in the full light of the moon, they heard a shot fired and a shout in Turkish, and Mahmoud reined in his horse and shouted back and said to Bates. "My people, the Nizam. You wait here, I see."

He spurred his horse and rode swiftly, shouting out, toward a high earthwork that lay to the west of them, and they waited and cursed the delay. In a little while Mahmoud came riding back and said, grinning, "The Turkish Army is holding the ridge now, but the Russians are all around us."

Bales frowned. "The Turkish Army? On the ridge? There are no defenses here, how can they hold it? And how many of them?"

Mahmoud teeth were gleaming in his dark, weather-beaten face. "Eight, nine hundred men; two, three guns, but old guns, no good. They take them from Ingles ships in the harbor."

Bates murmured. "The twelve-pounders. And eight

hundred men won't stop the whole Russian Army. Are they dug in there?"

Mahmoud shrugged. "Four barricades of beaten earth, that is all."

"Lord stone the crows! How are they going to stop twenty thousand Russkies, can you tell me that? Did you find out where the British are?"

Mahmoud pointed. "They are still on the upland, over by Sapoune and north of the road."

"And the main Russian force?"

Mahmoud shrugged. "Who can tell? They think they are to the east, at the head of the North Valley, and on the banks of the Tchernaya. But the South Valley, too, it is full of patrols."

Bates said, scowling, "In other words, this is all enemy-held territory, except for the upland. That's not a good prospect, friend."

"So better we ride north some more, then turn to the west until we can ride past them."

They moved off across the wide ridge and when they turned to the west, once more they ran into the Cossacks. Five, six, eight hundred of them were advancing along the north lee of the ridge, taking advantage of the gentle rise to hide their movements from the Turks above them. They turned their horses and rode hard to the east.

And when the very first signs of the dawn were in the sky, they found themselves in the small open plain to the north of Canrobert Hill. Bates swore softly and said, "There, at Kamara, the only safe place for us now..."

They wheeled their horses and galloped fast, and they did not stop until they had reached the heights. They urged their ponies on, moving quickly over the broken sandstone rocks, seeking out the shelter of the mountain that would shield them from all the deadly forces in the valley below.

It was like a game of chess in the darkness down there.

THE CHARGE OF THE LIGHT BRIGADE

They had ridden, they knew, hard on the tail of the enemy, and the enemy had ridden on their tail too. The valleys and the plain belonged to the fighting men, of both sides, who were scouring the landscape with weapons in their hands and death on their minds.

They found a hidden place at last, high in the hills, with a steep cliff above them to shelter them from the wind, and a small spring to give them water. Exhausted by the night's riding, they lay down in the sand, covered themselves with their ragged blankets, and uneasily slept away the few remaining moments of the night.

Once, Kirk woke to find Jenny pressing herself close to him for warmth in her sleep. She stirred while he looked at her and wondered if she felt as lost and as lonely as he did. He found a coat and covered her with it, and she opened her eyes and looked at him solemnly, and then closed them again as he lay once more close beside her, his arm across her frail body. The sky was already bright in the east, with long low lines of brilliant copper against the gray mountains.

And then came the sound of the first cannonade.

CHAPTER 9

It was the morning of October 25, and the assault guns were beginning to fire again. Only now they were Russian guns.

The sun had not yet risen over the mountains, and the light was cold and gray. Shivering under the thin, ragged blanket where he lay on the sand in the lee of the cliffs, Kirk raised himself and listened. He looked at Jenny close beside him; her troubled face restful in sleep, she lay with one arm across his chest. Gently, he moved it aside, adjusted the coat over her, and knelt there for a moment, listening. The birds were shrilling loudly, as though the cannonade had dared to disturb their country serenity. Somewhere, the thin note of a trumpet hung in the air.

He looked around for Bates, but the old man was not there, Epernon, close by, was rubbing the sleep from his eyes, rousing himself, and the Turks were stirring, eight of them waking from heavy sleep and shivering.

Kirk moved over to Epernon, crawling along the ground. "Our guns? Or theirs?"

"*Les Russes*," Epernon said, "Now, perhaps, comrades, yours and mine, will at last understand that they are to be attacked. Now it is their turn to stand and defend themselves."

THE CHARGE OF THE LIGHT BRIGADE

The guns were thundering loudly, a heavy bombardment of shells and cannonball, interspersed with controlled volleys of musket fire.

But it was neither the British nor the French who were under attack. Along the ridge that went from east to west through the center of the Tchernaya Plain, along the Causeway Heights that carried the road to Yalta, four hundred Turks had been sent by Lord Raglan—four hundred of the thousand who were scattered over the plain—to hold the earthen redoubts and stand till they perished should the unlikely report of the spies be true, and should the Russians actually dare to attack. It had not seemed likely to His Lordship that the reports of the Bashi-Bazouk could be correct, where the reports of Sir George Cathcart's scouting party had been so completely negative. And, when he was at last persuaded to set out a defensive line to cover his rear, it did not occur to him that should the enemy attack, perhaps as many as thirty thousand of them, a mere four hundred Turks behind inadequate defenses would not really be able to stop them.

The British sappers had dug the four redoubts, two on each side of the road and spaced half a mile or so apart. Here the Turks had been given two old naval twelve-pounders, and with three more of the ancient guns another seven or eight hundred Turks had occupied the eminence known as "Canrobert's Hill" three-quarters of a mile to the south, a small hillock in the plain that was, at this moment, dominated by the Russian guns.

The Causeway was some five miles long and a little over half a mile wide at its widest point. Though its height was not great, the slight rise gave the defenders a field of fire which could have been an embarrassment to the Russians in their march against Balaklava, and General Menshikov had ordered that the Turkish-manned guns be captured. He had detached a force of 2,500 men from his main body and ordered them to throw the Turks off the Causeway and take the guns down to the head of the North Valley where his main forces wore now stationed.

Lacking any support at all from their Allies, 170 Turks were killed before they prudently withdrew under the heavy bombardment. Under artillery fire and constant charges of the cavalry, they broke their fragile line and fled, retreating down the slope to the south into the South Valley and beyond it.

And the way was now open for the major Russian attack on the French and British positions.

Bates had climbed up to the top of the peak at the sound of the first barrage. They saw him standing there on the skyline, poised high above them, looking down on the plain. Jenny was stirring, and she sat up suddenly in fright and said, "What is it, has it started?"

Kirk bent to her and knelt on the ground beside her. He said, "The Russians have opened their attack. But we're safe here, no harm will come to you."

She threw aside the coat and stumbled to her feet, tripping over her long dress. He put out his arms to help her, holding her for a moment, feeling the sleep warmth of her body. Her eyes were red-rimmed, her face smeared with dust and dirt. He felt close to her, and as a stranger to the Bashi-Bazouk around him who were, he knew, his friends. It was as though there were just the two of them lost in an alien desert. He gestured toward Bates up there on the heights and said, "Come, we'll see what there is to see."

He took her hand and they climbed together up the steep rise. Epernon was ahead of them, and he turned round and grinned, and held out a hand for Jenny when she reached him, and he said, "Two ways, are there not, to witness a battle. From up here, or from down there." He grinned quickly. "It is better up here, believe me. There will be many dead men in the valley today."

THE CHARGE OF THE LIGHT BRIGADE

Behind them, the Turks were putting out their fires, rolling up their blankets, finishing off the scraps of last night's meal, taking their time and not hurrying, because the sound of the guns was far away, across the other side of the ridge and far below them. The site for the battle had been chosen now, and it was not here. They had chosen a crows' nest for a refuge, and the battle ground was spread out below them, distant and detached and somehow puny.

They reached the top where Bates was, and he turned and touched his forehead to Jenny and said politely, "Did you sleep well, Ma'am?"

She did not answer. She was staring out onto the plain that lay like a sand table dressed for their inspection, the North and the South Valleys separated by the Causeway, the small mound of Canrobert's Hill, the Fedioukine Hills and the Tchernaya River far to the north, with Kadikoi village a tiny speck to the west, and the Sapoune Ridge and the uplands high above it. They could see the road that led to Balaklava, a sandy white ribbon stretched out across the plain. And they could see, between the ridge and the Fedioukine Hills, the great black rectangles of the Russian forces at the head of the North Valley, their massed guns pointed down the valley to the east. Three miles or so to the west of them, and a little to the south, they could see the British cavalry on the southern side of Sapoune Ridge, moving down slowly from the uplands, toward the enemy.

Closer in, there were tiny black ants running down the slope of the Causeway, heading across the South Valley, heading for Balaklava, and Bates pointed and said, "The Turks. They're running."

And now, the first great phalanx of Russian cavalry came breasting up over the ridge, more than a thousand of them riding in extended order and wielding their sabers, crossing the road and pouring down the other side, hard on the heels of the fleeing

Turks. They saw men fall from musket fire and exploding shells and then the Russians wheeled land retreated, galloping fast back up onto the Causeway and down the other side once more.

Epernon pointed, "There, in the grass, above Kadikoi, you see?"

Kirk stared. South of the Causeway, there were touches of color in the green grass, like scattered poppies that had not been there before, a long thin line of scarlet and green and yellow and blue that was now moving. Bates said, scowling, "A naval eyeglass, I should have stolen one."

The Russians were charging up over the ridge again, cutting their way once more among the fleeing Turks. And still the British were moving slowly down toward them.

Kirk said, aghast, "For God's sake, where are they heading? Can't they see the Russkies there?"

Bates shook his head. "That's just it, boy. Is plain enough from up here, but they're cut off from any sight of them down there. The ground's not as flat as it looks."

Kirk said, mumbling, "The Inniskillings and the Grays and the Dragoons, the Heavy Brigade." He stared and pointed, and said excitedly, "And the Light Brigade beyond them, you see?" They were wheeling round to the north, moving away from the Heavies and taking up a position at the eastern end of the North Valley.

There were four squares of cavalry moving down from the uplands to the south of the ridge—the Inniskillings and the Scots Grays on the left, the Fourth and Fifth Dragoons on the right, the whole of the Heavy Brigade in all its colorful splendor.

Kirk said again, "My God..." He looked at Bates in alarm: "The whole Russian Army's on their flank, Jack!"

Hidden from the British by the wide curve of the ridge, the Russians had re-formed their squadrons and were moving fast across the South Valley. And now, out of the gray-green grass, the thin line of bright colors rose with startling suddenness. It

THE CHARGE OF THE LIGHT BRIGADE

was the ninety-third Highlanders rising up out of the ground where they had lain since daybreak.

Far, far beyond them, on the edge of Sapoune Ridge, there were other spectators. Here, the merchants, the servants, the hangers-on, and the officers' wives had set up a little camp to watch the Heavy Brigade going into action.

Some of the officers had sent horses down to the harbor for their wives in the first light, when the guns had opened their cannonade, telling them that the battle was soon to begin and not to wait for breakfast. They were all here now, watching the spectacle excitedly from a point of comfortable vantage, sitting in camp chairs or on the blankets on the ground, watching the splendor of their men going in to do battle with the Russians; some of them were taking their morning tea. This was what they had so long ago left their distant homes for, to watch the destruction, once and for all, of the arrogant Czar's ambitious armies. It was to be a spectacle for them, a circus for their pleasure.

And now, now you could hear the sound of the muskets as the Highlanders fired. The thin line of bright tartan colors, standing in knee-deep grass, was directly in line with the advancing Russians, reining in their horses now, startled by the unexpected appearance of five hundred determined men in their path. But only for a moment...

Up on the peak, they could hear the yelling as the Russians saw the miniscule scope of the threat and charged the thin bright line. The Highlanders fired, and reloaded and fired their ancient muskets (most of them had scorned the new Minié rifles and preferred the old muskets which had always served them so well), and reloaded and fired again, and again, and again.

Many of them fell from the Russian bullets, but the line held firm and did not waver. The Russians wheeled back and charged again, and still the line held. The valley was thick with dead horses and riders, and now the Russians broke off the attack and rode back up the hill in headlong retreat. From the peak, the watchers could see them regrouping on the other side of the Ridge. And still, the Heavy Brigade was moving slowly down the slope into position.

Kirk said bitterly, "Even if they'd seen the Highlanders, they'd have been too late to help them. My God, they must have heard the firing what in God's name were they wailing for? And where the devil's the Light Brigade?"

Bates shrugged. "They were waiting, I'll be bound, for orders. And the Highlanders held, Kirk, did you see? But keep your eyes on the Inniskillings, they're riding into a trap."

To the left of the four squares of the Brigade, a single man was riding, a squat, thick-set figure on a fine gray horse, holding himself straight and light in the saddle in spite of his bulk.

Kirk said, "Scarlett, General Scarlett, one of the best. One of the few best, he's a good man."

Epernon said drily, "Is he good enough to know the enemy is less than a mile away from his flank, ready to move in for the kill?"

Kirk muttered angrily, and Bates said, "Nothing you can do from up here, boy, the battle'll be over before we could even get down to the plain. And chances are they've got scouts up on the ridge there where they can see what's happening."

Kirk shook his head. "No. No the Heavy Brigade, not the cavalry. They'll ride straight ahead and dare the devil himself to stop them, to hell with what's on their flanks."

Jenny said, "Helplessness, is a terrible thing to suffer... Is there nothing we can do but watch?"

Bates said calmly, "Nothing, Ma'am. Just thank the Lord for our own safety. That's the ground you've been wandering around in like a lost soul, and soon there won't be a living man down there with a soul left to call his own."

THE CHARGE OF THE LIGHT BRIGADE

And now, they saw the Russians move up once move toward the top of the rise, walking their horses, two great solid masses of cavalry. They had changed their direction now, a little to the west, and when they breasted the rise, they stopped. It seemed from up on the peak as though they were looking down on the Brigade that was moving slowly across their line of march, less than a mile ahead of them.

For a brief moment, they paused. And then they charged. The sound of their fierce yelling was brought to those on the peak, and they stood and watched helplessly as the cavalry horde poured over the ridge and down into the South Valley. They were swooping down onto the flank of the Heavy Brigade, to the left of the Scots Grays and the Inniskillings.

Kirk sucked in his breath. "It's not good to watch your own men being cut to pieces."

Jenny's hand was to her face, and Epernon looked at her and said; "There'll be many bodies for you to patch up when this is all over, Mam'selle."

Now, down there the Heavy Brigade at last saw the threat to their left; they could not, at this close range, have avoided seeing it. They saw General Scarlett raise his sword, and the whole Brigade wheeled left.

Bates said, "Watch, Kirk. Watch and learn a lesson."

The Heavy Brigade wheeled to face the heights.

And now, the general calmly turned his back on the advancing enemy and gave the order for the lines to be dressed. The officers turned their backs too and called out the orders. The four squares of cavalry lined up in precise formation, the bright reds und blues of their uniforms a splash of splendid color against the grass, their leatherwork shining, their pipe clay immaculate, their brasses glistening in the early morning sun, the horses prancing. And the enemy thundered down the slope toward them, more than 2,500 of them swooping down in a thick gray mass of thundering hooves.

The officers, their backs to the Russians, sat their horses and waited for the lines to finish their dressing, sat there immobile and unhurried. And when, at last, the orders were completed and the lines were in precise and immaculate formation, only then did the officers turn their horses to face the onrush of the charging Russians, who were now less than four hundred yards away, and coming on fast, their lances held low, their sabers ready.

To the two leading Regiments, the Grays and the Inniskillings, General Scarlett called out the order: "Sound the charge!"

He did not wait for the order to be carried out. He spurred his horse and headed at a gallop straight for the advancing Russian lines. His aide-de-camp, his orderly, and his own trumpeter took off at speed with him, and the four men hurled themselves headlong at the great mass of the enemy.

But the rest of them... This was not the way the drill books had taught them. (England had not been at war for forty years, and few of the soldiers had any battle experience at all.) They knew that the charge is an orderly progression of events: first the walk, then the trot, then the gallop, and only after these steps have been completed can the final charge be sounded. And so, by the time the regimental trumpeters had at last sounded the charge, General Scarlett and his three men had reached, alone, the Russian lines. The aide-de-camp ran his sword through the leading Russian officer and hurled him from his horse, and then the four of them were hitting the first of the Russian ranks head-on. They drove deep into the solid phalanx of massed horsemen, whirling their swords like dervishes. Only then, deep in among the enemy, did they wheel their horses to see the regiments advancing in their wake.

And now, the Inniskillings and the Grays began their furious, masterly, and chaotic fight. The odds against them were a little under ten to one, but the Russians, ill-drilled and badly

THE CHARGE OF THE LIGHT BRIGADE

disciplined, were too tightly packed for easy maneuvering. Scarlett's three hundred, all mounted on heavy horses of sixteen hands or more, were head and shoulders above the lighter-mounted Russians, though—incredible as it may seem—the Brigade had come unprepared for close fighting and were not wearing their protective shoulder scales. They cut their way with their sabers deep into the enemy lines, whirling their swords and wheeling their heavy horses, slashing to right and left and ahead and behind.

And now, the waiting Dragoons took up the fight. In four squadrons, the Fourth and the Fifth charged at the enemy flanks, two squadrons on the right, one on the left, and one more hard on the heels of the opening attack.

Five hundred yards away, the Light Brigade stood in precise formation and watched the battle, waiting for orders to join it. Nobody gave those orders. Their commander, Lord Cardigan, sat his horse ramrod-stiff and watched; even the horses were fidgeting impatiently.

The Heavy Brigade fought on. For ten minutes they cut and thrust and wheeled their horses and cut and thrust again. And then, the Russians broke. There was a wavering first at the front, and the fronts ranks pressed back upon the rear. And then the rear ranks broke (some of the Inniskillings and Grays had cut their way, right through them and were behind them now), and the whole mass of the enemy broke off the battle and fled. They galloped hard up the ridge to the Causeway and down the other side into the safety of the North Valley.

Seventy-eight British cavalrymen lay dead on the field, and 490 Russians. But the assault on Balaklava, for this is what the Russians had meant it to be, was over.

Kirk stared. He said, his face taut with anger and dismay, "The Light Brigade, what in God's name were they waiting for? Why didn't they charge?"

Bates shook his head. "Your Army, Kirk, not mine. In the

Navy, one ship comes to the help of another."

No help had come to the hard-pressed Heavy Brigade because no one saw fit to give the necessary order. It was simple enough. Lord Cardigan (who was soon to redeem himself in good measure) had been given somewhat ambiguous. instructions. He had been told not to leave his position but to attack anything and everything that came within his reach. History has not yet decided whether a major battle less than five hundred yards from his position should be construed as "within reach." The orders had come from his immediate superior, Lord Lucan, who was Cardigan's brother-in-law and an old enemy.

Kirk said angrily, "It's not my Army any more, Jack." He did not sound very sure of himself. He climbed painfully to his feet and stood for a moment looking down at Jenny. She was still staring off at the battlefield, and he knew that she was thinking of the dead and the wounded down there. He said bitterly, "Take your fill of the war, Miss Enderly." She looked at him sharply but said nothing. He moved off down the hill toward the little shelter where the fires had been.

Jenny looked at Bates. "Go to him, Bates," she said urgently. "You know what it is that's troubling him."

"Aye. It's what's troubling all of us. Only Kirk hasn't the strength to face it, not yet. The tide's washing over him, and he's not the power in his arms to hold it back, nor even to swim with it. But, he'll learn. The day will come when he'll know exactly where it's carrying him."

"And then?"

Epernon said, "Then, he will be ready for his death. That is the only moment at which we know just how much sense there is in the shape of things."

Bates turned to move down the hill. Then he turned back and said in a moment: "Come with me, Miss Enderly. I've a feeling he needs more than I can give him."

Silently she got up and moved down with him.

THE CHARGE OF THE LIGHT BRIGADE

They found Kirk sitting dejectedly on a ledge, his head sunk in his hands. They sat beside him and said nothing, just letting him feel the comfort of their company.

Below them, the now empty field was pin-pointed with dark and colored splashes that were bodies, bodies of men and horses lying together where the fighting had been. To the north of the Causeway they could see the Russians dragging away the Turkish guns, laboring them slowly to the positions where their own guns were, at the head of the North Valley that was not really a valley at all but merely an opening between the Fedioukine Hills and the Causeway, with the river curling round on its northeast flank. And at the other, the western, end of the valley, the Light Brigade was lining up into position, dressing its ranks. To the east, a little under two miles away, the great masses of the Russians were behind their own cannons, and the Turkish guns, late off the ships of the British Navy, were being trundled on their useless little wooden wheels toward them, down the slope of the Causeway that was three-quarters of a mile to their left.

Bates said, struggling for the right words, "You watch your men fighting, and you long to be with them. Is it for this that you left the Army? That you became a deserter?"

"A deserter? Yes, that's what I am now, in full measure. Is it any good telling you it's not really what I wanted to be?"

"Aye, I can understand that. A man sometimes gets pushed into what he doesn't really want, though not fighting it at the right time. And once the decision's been made for him, there's nary a great deal he can do about it. Except ride with it, Kirk."

"There are better things for a young man," Jenny said urgently, "than being blown to pieces in a useless battle. For that's what it is, useless! Do you think it'll change the course of history? When I was a child, half my family were killed off fighting the French, and now...now it's the Russians. Even if we win this war, who will it be tomorrow?"

Kirk sighed. "Aye, there's no use to it all, and that's the truth. But the truth itself isn't enough, we're not wise enough to accept it for what it is. We look at the sugarcoating around it, the sugarcoating that's the glory and the splendor. You saw it yourself. It was a fine thing they did down there."

"Yes, fine for those who survived it." Jenny put out a hand and touched his arm. "But when the night comes and it's all over, I'll be down there again, and I'll not be dealing with those who survived. I'll be searching the field for the mutilated and the helpless...just as your friends found you at the Alma, Kirk. You served well there, and isn't that enough for one man's lifetime?" He did not answer, and she said urging him. "At first, I thought you were wrong, deserter is an ugly word, but now...now, I don't know any more. When I see the eagerness in your face to be down there and die among them... I just don't know any more. Perhaps you were right after all."

"Right to desert?"

She said tightly, "If that's what you want to call it, yes, you were right to desert, I'd rather call it...a withdrawal. There comes a time to do that too, you know. The fear of death... I've seen enough of it, I know what it can do to a man."

Kirk shook his head stubbornly. "Not fear of death. I'll die for my country, for my friends too if I have to. But it's got to be done the right way, with the decisions made by the man who's to die. At the Alma we stood under their fire and let them cut us to ribbons, and for what? Can you tell me that?"

Bates said gently, "It was a bitter battle, and a foolish one. But we won, didn't we?"

"And down there too, in the valley, they put their heads down and charged blindly, with no reason at all, their eyes shut and their swords waving, three hundred men against near three thousand, and for what?"

"And still," Bates said, insisting, "still, they won again,

THE CHARGE OF THE LIGHT BRIGADE

the way they always do. Doesn't that mean something to you?"

"Aye, it's that that worries me. It means that maybe *they* are right after all. Is that what war's about, Jack? That the likes of you and me should accept it blindly, not asking why but doing as we're told? Maybe they *do* know better than we do. Maybe that's what it's all about. Maybe we're wrong, all of us, you and Frenchy and me."

Jenny leaned in closer to him. She said, "Think of the living, Kirk, not of the dead. All right, they're still alive, to take their chances again. But how long can they go on doing that? Are all our young men to be killed off in a war that's never going to end?"

He looked at her strangely. "Are you on my side, Jenny, if I make the wrong choice too? A while back you were telling me to go back to my regiment...and I tried to, I tried hard. I left my friends here and I went back to them, and they would have had me shot for a deserter. A broken leg, a bullet in the shoulder, and still they'd shoot me. I felt the shame of it."

He looked round to find Epernon standing behind him; he had not heard him approach. He looked away, waiting for Jenny to answer him.

She said at last, "Yes, I'm on your side now Kirk, whatever you chose to do. The choice is yours. I'll be happy if you stay out of it."

"And when it's all over, what then? Go where? Live... how?"

Epernon sat down beside them. He said with a laugh, "We will live in this God-forsaken country, because not one of us can ever go to his home again."

Kirk turned to him. "Did you think of that when you chose to desert?"

"Yes, I did. And the specter was a terrible one. For a man of quality, this is a very limited country. Yes, I thought of that."

Kirk said fiercely, "Then why?"

Epernon shrugged. "It is human nature to think wisely and act foolishly. Does that answer your question?"

Kirk turned to Bates. "And you, Jack? Is that enough for you too?"

Bates laughed. He said, "It's enough that I've made the choice, yes, because there's no going back on it, so accept it. But if I had second thoughts... I don't know. Maybe if I'd stopped to think a little longer... The question is, isn't it, do we fight or don't we? When I was a young man, fighting the French, I was full of fire and energy, and I knew that I was right, that we were doing the right thing, because if we hadn't fought, we'd all be part of Prince Louis Empire now, and Frenchy here would be lording it over us all in London. So, maybe the war was right then, and if it was right then, it must be right now, wouldn't you say? But we're a long way from home out here, and there's no Napoleon about to invade us, not as far as I can see, and if it's a fight over who should have rights to the Dardanelles out there, which is what it is, then maybe we should have no part of it."

Kirk said moodily, "You're not being much help, Jack"

And Bates told him gently, "I'm saying, boy, that the decision has got to be yours. Just do what you think is right, and if it's wrong, then learn to live with it. The way I did. Cast your die, boy, and don't whine at the way it comes up. Lord stone the crows! Your fate's in your own hands, nobody else's."

Jenny sat there, somber and silent. As he looked at her now, Kirk felt a strange and uneasy longing for her. He looked out across the rolling hills and the plain, and he said slowly:

"My home is like this, the same rolling downs... They'll be harvesting there now, and the rabbits will be running out from the standing wheat, and there's the smell of hay... We used to run down the rabbits and take them home for supper, and... I made a pair of gloves, once, out of rabbit skins... I used to walk through the fields at night, after the wheat was cut, just for the sake of the smell of it..."

He broke off staring moodily down at the ground, and Epernon said gently, "Your home is here now, my friend. You are one of us. You are a Bashi-Bazouk."

"No, I'm not. I never will be."

He felt Jenny's hand tighten on his arm. He looked at her and took her hand in his. In a little while, Bates and Epernon got up and moved away and left the two of them siting there on a high ledge overlooking the immensity of the land below, sitting there and holding hands, like lovers.

CHAPTER 10

The critical area was the gentle grass-covered narrow plain that had become known as the North Valley.

The valley was some two miles long, and at its narrowest point less than half a mile wide. Its northern flank was the high mass of the Fedioukine Hills, and here, the Russians had stationed fourteen guns, with four cavalry squadrons and eight battalions of infantry. Its southern flank was the long line of the Causeway Heights. Here, a Russian infantry regiment with a field battery of artillery was moving westward along the ridge to take up its position. Here, too, the naval guns they had captured from the Turks were still being slowly trundled down the hills.

These two strong forces looked down into the North Valley from commanding and fluid positions on either side of it.

And to the eastern end of the valley, the main Russian forces were waiting, cavalry and infantry in battle order, more than twenty thousand of them drawn up in dense and massive squares. A line of twelve guns was being drawn across the front of their positions. The valley was thus a funnel, its sides and one end firmly held by the Russians in force, and at its other, eastern end, the men of the Light Brigade calmly sat their horses and waited for someone to give them some orders. Without orders

THE CHARGE OF THE LIGHT BRIGADE

they could not move, and their last instructions had been to hold their position and to strike only at anything within reach.

On the raised plateau of the upland, where the commander and his staff had taken up a point of vantage, Lord Raglan could clearly see the disposition of his own men and those of the enemy; it seemed that both sides were waiting for something to happen. It was obvious to him that the war, for the time being at least, had moved from the South Valley into the North. And it was also obvious to him that the naval guns which the Turks had lost would soon be added to the twelve guns which the Russians had drawn across their front.

He sent down an order, written hastily on a scrap of paper: "Lord Raglan wishes the cavalry to advance rapidly to the front and to prevent the enemy carrying away the guns." It was sent down to the Light Brigade by his aide-de-camp, Captain Nolan, a young and arrogant officer of the Seventeenth Lancers, an expert cavalryman and a good soldier.

For a long time, Kirk had not spoken.

The others had gone, Bates and Epernon, and the Turks had gone back to the hollow to light a fire and cook some food and then sleep, for there was nothing for them to do now; the searching and scouting and patrolling was over, and all that was left now was for the two great forces down there to clash and decide, once and for all, what this war was going to achieve.

They would sleep for the rest of the morning, secure on their remote and craggy mountain, and in the evening they would ride out again to see what they could find on the battlefield when the battle was done. There would be English gold to steal and Russian throats to cut, but for now, some sleep was all that was needed.

With an almost mechanical motion, Kirk began to strip off what was left of his leatherwork, the crossed breast straps and the wide belt. He took off his torn jacket and stared for a while at the once-bright buttons that were now tarnished and blackened. He sat there moodily, the flesh of his chest white in the early morning sun, and then he took off his boots as well, and unwrapped the rags that were round his feet.

He stood up then, and looked down at Jenny and said simply, "I know what I've got to do, but... I don't know the reasons why. Can you tell me, Jenny?"

She looked at him. "Is it perhaps because of me, Kirk?"

"Perhaps."

"Whatever you decide, you'll not lose my respect, one way or another."

"Perhaps it's more than that that I'm looking for."

"Is it, Kirk? Is it?"

"I don't know, Jenny, I wish I could be sure." He sighed and said: "Will you wait here for me?"

He walked away while she stared after him, and went down to the rocks where the Turks were, and she saw him pull out the knife from the scabbard at his waist and carve a piece of the roasting meat that was lying on the hot stones there, and then he came back and sat beside her, and began rubbing the fat slowly over the leather.

Wanting to break the uneasy silence, he said, making a joke of it, "I used to have the best leather in the outfit, and look at it now."

She did not smile. Instead, she took the coat he had laid there and began to rub some of the dirt off it, twisting the cloth to loosen the packed mud and shaking it free. Her young, eager face had lost its liveliness, and her eyes were dulled.

He sat cross-legged, like a Turk, beside her as he worked. In a little while, the leather took on a dull sheen, and he said, "A soft brush and some soap, and it could still shine again, just as it used to." He laid it across his knee and began buffing it with the heel of his hand. He looked at the jacket in her lap; the broad white bars across its front, eight wide straps in pairs from the waist to the chest, were the color of the red-gray soil now, and he said, "I wish I could find some chalk, I could make them white again."

But there was only sandstone here, sandstone and gravel and red-black earth, and Jenny shook her head and said, "It's the heart that beats under all this, that's what's important. The rest is just...dressing. It's the sugarcoating over the truth that you spoke of."

"Aye. And it's good to know that it's still there."

She knew that what he was doing was right, but she said, nonetheless, "Are you sure, Kirk? Are you sure this is what you want?"

"Aye. It's what I want, and it's what you want too, isn't it?"

Not knowing, she shook her head. "And after?"

He shrugged. "I'll face what comes after when I have to."

As though helping him find an excuse to weaken, she said, "Your leg? You still can't put any weight on it."

"I won't have to. I can ride, and that's all that matters. I can ride, and I've a good sword, and it's my own people who'll be with me again."

He wrapped his foot rags carefully round his feet and put on the boots, and tied the broken thong laces in small knots to hold them firm, cutting off the ends of them with his knife and taking his time about making them as tidy as possible, and she stood up and held out the proud, tattered coat for him. Three of the buttons had gone, and it was loose and hanging on him now. He put on the crossbelts and felt instinctively for his pack, knowing that it was a reflex movement that meant he was a soldier again, even though all his equipment was still down there, no doubt, with thousands of other wasted pieces on the banks of the Alma where he had lost it.

He felt the inch-long stubble of beard on his chin, and

said, "They'd fog me if I came on parade like this. That was one of the things that always made me hate them, the floggings and the cruelty, but maybe that's what makes a good soldier. Maybe they'd be right to do that, wouldn't they? We are an Army, not a rabble, the proudest Army that England has ever seen. The scum of the earth, the Duke of Wellington called us, and he was right too. But we win our battles because we do as we are told, because we do as *they* tell us without questioning them. Maybe that's all were good for."

Jenny said gently, "It won't always be like that, Kirk."

"No, maybe not. But that's the way it is now, and that's what I'll accept. Bates and Frenchy, they've bought their freedom. But for me...the price is too high, Jenny. It's just too high." He looked at her and said again, "Will you wait for me? I'll see the old man before I go. He's been a good friend."

She nodded. He turned away from her and walked slowly up the hill.

He found Bates and Epernon sitting with Mahmoud on an outcrop of rocks and staring down onto the plain below them, the whole vast panorama of the Crim Tartary spread out down there for their inspection, a carpet of green and brown crisscrossed with sandy roads and patched with small farms, with the rivers winding lazily through them. Even the horsemen drawn up there in battle order and the great masses of infantry as far as they could see could not destroy the illusion of a perfect peace. The guns were silent now; they could see the dispatch-riders, on both sides urging their horses fast across the plains, each on his private errand. They saw the naval guns on their little wheels being manhandled, still, down the slope of the Causeway toward the main body of the Russian forces.

Bates looked at Kirk without surprise, and Epernon said softly, "So the time has come, soldier... If you want a razor, Mahmoud here has a sharp knife."

Kirk shook his head and held out his hand. "I came to tell

you goodbye. And to thank you for all you have done for me."

Bates took his hand. "You're a fine lad, Kirk, and I'm sorry you'll be leaving us. But I know that you would, sooner or later. And your young Miss Enderly?"

Kirk sighed. "Not mine, Jack. She could have been, perhaps, if things had turned out different. And one day, maybe, when this is all over..." He remembered that he had not told her about her medallion. He said, "We might meet again someday, somewhere. I hope that we do."

"And if not... Good luck, boy. You'll have a hard time explaining your long absence, you know that?"

"Aye, I know it. If I can prove myself before I have too..."

He took Epernon's hand, and the Frenchman said, "You exchange your freedom for slavery, Kirk. But no one of us will deny you the right to choose your own destiny. And when they shoot you down as a deserter, let your last thoughts be of us—free men."

Kirk: said, "Perhaps you've earned your freedom. And perhaps it isn't really that at all. Goodbye."

Mahmoud was moving in on them, looking at the uniform with surprise on his face. He stood a little below them, watching, and Kirk turned to him and smiled and said, "Will you give me the bay mare with the white hocks, Mahmoud? The fastest horse we have."

Mahmoud nodded gravely. "A present for you, now that you are a man again. Take her with Allah's blessing. But watch for the guns, for she turns always toward them. Her name is Mandoh which means, in your language, speed. A good horse. I add my blessing to Allah's."

They shook hands, and Kirk turned sharply away and went back to where Jenny was waiting for him. He put his arms round her and kissed her and said, "Go down with them to Balaklava, Bates will take you there."

"No, I'll stay here with them. For a while, at least."

He was surprised. "With the Bashi-Bazouk?"

"Until the battle is over. Tonight I'll be down there on the field, helping in the only way I can. After that...who knows?"

"I have a feeling there'll be plenty of work for you down there."

"Perhaps."

He wanted to tell her about the medallion, and he stumbled on the words and said: "When I saw you that day...you dropped your medallion, the little gold one, you know?"

She waited, watching him.

He said, "I found it."

Her voice was pleased. She said eagerly, "Keep it then, it will bring you luck. I want you to keep it."

"All right." He did not dare tell her what had become of it. "And will you...will you think of me sometimes?"

She hesitated. "You speak as though we'll never meet again."

"Who knows? I can only think, now, of the next few hours. There is a lot to be decided in that little time, Jenny."

"Then...when you get back to your lines, after the battle is over, will you look for me?"

He said gravely, "I will look for you."

He held her tightly and kissed her again, and when one of the Turks came up, grinning at them and leading the bay horse whose name was Mandoh, he pulled away and held both her hands for a moment, and then climbed heavily onto the horse and sat straight in the saddle and looked down at her and said, "One day, somewhere, if there's a God in Heaven..."

She did not answer.

He turned his mount and moved slowly down the hill, heading for the South Valley, heading for the Causeway and over it into the North Valley, heading for the distant group of horsemen that were his comrades in the Light Brigade.

THE CHARGE OF THE LIGHT BRIGADE

* * *

Captain Nolan was riding fast down the steep slope of the mountain. There was a track that followed the contours of the land, but he scorned to use it. An excellent rider who prided himself on his cavalry expertise, he took the sheer drop down the cliff instead, riding at breakneck speed, the highly trained horse slipping down on its haunches and slithering to the bottom. He galloped hard up the eastern end of the Causeway, across the other side into the North Valley, and handed his message to Lord Lucan.

It is pertinent to record that this instruction, written so carelessly on a scrap of paper, became known to history as "Raglan's fourth order." And there is no doubt that the reference to "the guns" was a matter of some ambiguity, since there were now two sets of enemy guns on the battlefield—the defensive guns which the Russians had drawn across their front, and the guns they had captured from the Turks on the Causeway. The words "Carrying away" perhaps should have indicated clearly which guns His Lordship was referring to, and his third order (which no one had seen fit to act upon) had stated quite clearly that the cavalry's objective was to be the recovery of the heights which the Turks had lost, the Causeway that flanked the valley on the south. The fourth order, following closely on the third, *ought* to have indicated that the guns under reference were those being trundled down from the heights, and not the ones that stood in front of the massive Russian positions.

But there is no excuse for ambiguity when the lives of men are at stake. History has also recorded that Lucan did, in fact, query the instruction, and that Nolan—close to Lord Raglan and, therefore, well aware of his intentions—swept his arm in a gesture that can only be described as indefinite, toward the eastern end of the North Valley and answered, "There, my Lord, are your guns..." Where upon Lord Lucan rode off to see his brother-in-law, Lord Cardigan, and read the commander's order to him.

"Allow me to point out," Cardigan is reported to have answered coldly, "that the Russians have a battery in the valley to our front, and batteries and riflemen on each flank."

Lord Lucan shrugged and repeated Raglan's order, Cardigan said no more. He posted himself at the head of his men, facing down the funnel of the valley. And now, he gave the order:

"The Brigade will advance at the walk!"

The front line of the Brigade was made up of the Seventeenth Lancers and the Thirteenth Dragoons; the second line consisted of the Eleventh Hussars; and the third was formed by the Eighth Hussars and the Light Dragoons.

At the walk they moved off, their uniforms brilliant splashes of color, their dressing precise, their bearing immaculate. The light-weight horses trod the soft turf gently, as though they were on parade in Hyde Park or St. James'. And now, the next order in the accepted progression was given. Lord Cardigan raised his sword and called out:

"The Brigade will advance at the trot!"

Up to this moment, it could not have been obvious to anyone, not even to Lord Raglan and his staff from their commanding viewpoint on the uplands, that the Brigade was heading down the valley. It was quite possible, to any onlooker, that they were heading toward the valley's southern flank where the Turkish guns were being carried away. But, as they began to trot, it was immediately apparent that Lord Cardigan was taking them down the full length of the valley, under the guns on both sides and toward the massed guns at the eastern end. And at this point, Captain Nolan—who, on his own initiative, had now attached himself to his own Regiment, the Seventeenth Lancers—took it upon himself to break his position and gallop out fast to the head of the Brigade, even cutting across the general's own position. In normal times, this action would have earned him a court-martial, and his extraordinary behavior must have been dictated by sudden and pressing considerations.

He wheeled his horse, the Captain, and shouted out something which nobody heard, for now the Russians' guns had begun their deadly fire. A shell burst close by him, and a splinter pierced his spine, paralyzing him as he sat his horse, rigid and straight and with his sword still raised above his head. He screamed, a long-drawn-out and continuing scream, as his horse panicked and charged toward the oncoming Brigade, and when it galloped through their lines, Nolan swayed stiffly in his saddle, fell to the ground, and lay there. He was dead.

It was quite certain that he had realized, as the guns began to fire, that the Brigade was headed in the wrong direction, the only man on the field to know this, and now he was dead.

The Brigade trotted on, its dressing correct, the swords and lances ready, into the fire of the guns ahead of them, firing steadily now as the gunners reloaded and reloaded again.

Now, Lord Cardigan gave his next order:
"The Brigade will advance at the gallop!"

The riders spurred their horses in precise and automatic obedience, holding in their impatient horses. The cannons and the muskets were firing faster, on all sides of them, the fire from the heights on both flanks taking a deadly toll. The shells were bursting among the riders, and horses and men were falling, great bloodied gaps appearing in the ranks, and still the men maintained the controlled pace of the gallop. The final order for the charge had not yet been given.

The Brigade—what was left of it—moved on steadily. They could clearly see the cannons ahead of them now, their gaping mouths exploding with fire and steel, straight into their lines at point-blank range.

* * *

Now, on the flank, a solitary horseman was riding fast down the slope of the hill.

The little mare called Mandoh, lighter and faster even than the light-weight horses of the Light Brigade, was racing over the Causeway, her ears held flat, her nostrils flared and her eyes dilated. To her left along the ridge, the Russian infantry was firing down into the valley, and the mare pulled hard toward the sound of the guns. Kirk held a tight rein and urged the horse down the hill, whipping at her flank with the fat of his sword.

Ahead of him and to his left he could see the Light Brigade advancing at the gallop; in a moment now, he knew, the charge would be sounded. Ahead and to his right, the Russian guns were firing, the sun gleaming on the bright brass nozzles of the smoking cannons as the gunners worked feverishly, ramming home the shells with the long, heavy ramrods, and watching them burst, farther down the valley, among the onrushing cavalry. Their numbers were thinning out, but those who were still mounted pressed on.

The mare was swerving to the right now, and Kirk pulled hard on the left rein, trying to dig in his right ankle, Turkish fashion, and knowing that there was no strength in the leg at all. He swore and pulled harder on the reins, and the mare's head swung round. The Lancers were less than a hundred yards away now, and he saw a trooper turn to stare at him as he galloped forward, turned to stare at the ragged, dirty, unshaven figure who looked like one of the Bashi-Bazouk in stolen clothes, but riding his brightly caparisoned mare like a Lancer.

Kirk burst into the cavalry lines, swung his whole body over to the right to force the mare round, and gave Mandoh her head. The guns were no more than eighty yards ahead of them now, firing savagely. The charge had not been sounded, because there was no one left to sound it; and there was no attempt to hold formation now as the men urged their horses forward at breakneck speed, racing for the guns and their own destruction

THE CHARGE OF THE LIGHT BRIGADE

Some of the mounts were swinging away, their saddles empty. And of the 670 men who began the long ride down the North Valley, more than four hundred were out of action, dead, or dying, or wounded on the turf. And now the guns were under their noses, almost within reach of their swords.

Two hundred and thirty men, all that were left, charged into them. Thirty of them broke through into the battery, and two hundred fought their way past its flanks to the cavalry regiments of the Russians at the rear. Deep among the enemy, cutting their way in with a blind fury, they swung their swords and drove home their lances. They wheeled their horses and forced their way in and out, slashing at the tightly packed Russians, two hundred brightly uniformed men lost in the immense gray mass of twenty thousand. The Russian cavalry broke before the maniacal onslaught, unable to comprehend that less than two hundred horsemen were challenging the might of the entire Russian Army, the might of twenty thousand men drawn up in battle formation and protected by heavy guns. The two hundred drove their horses forward madly and wheeled and drove them again. For each man, the bodies all around him were enemy bodies, and wherever his sword might land it was in enemy flesh.

And now, at the western end of the valley, the Russians began to pour down from the Fedioukine Hills, behind the Light Brigade, seeking to cutoff any retreat by whatever survivors might be left. They headed east, along the North Valley, joining the fight, and the remnants of the Light Brigade turned, the front of the enemy broken, and charged back through the advancing lines, forcing a way once more through the enemy cavalry.

And, strewn along the valley floor, 270 men of the Light Brigade now lay dead, and 475 of their horses. The wounded were without number, because no one kept count of them.

The field and the guns were left to the Russians. They rode down among the stragglers and the wounded, cutting them down with their lances, shooting the wounded horses, picking their way among the littered dead; the ground was wet with blood.

And now, at last, the French moved in. Under Generals d'Alonville and Morris, the Chasseurs d'Afrique charged along the western end of the Fedioukine Hills and drove off the disorganized Russians.

But only temporarily. By the end of the day, the hills and the plains were once more firmly in Russian hands; and the Allies on the uplands had lost their lifeline to Balaklava. As a result 300,000 men were to die before Sebastopol should eventually fall, but for the moment, the battle for Balaklava was over.

Lord Cardigan, who had led the Light Brigades suicidal charge and had emerged from it, miraculously, unscathed, rode down to the harbor and to his yacht for a bath.

The valley was red with the blood of the dead and the dying.

CHAPTER 11

That evening, when the sun was sinking down over the uplands, they rode down from Kamara Hill into the North Valley below them.

Epernon and Mahmoud were riding fast, making repeated passes on the flanks, riding for half a mile ahead and then galloping back, as Bates carefully led Jenny's horse over the springy turf and the rough patches of red sandstone and gray-green earth. Gathered around them, all that were left of the Bashi-Bazouk, eighteen men in all, formed a bodyguard around the pair of them.

She sat her horse awkwardly, Jenny, riding astride like a man, with the long skirt wrapped around her legs; she held onto the pommel with both hands, and her face was white with a nameless fear.

They rode in silence.

The sun was setting when they reached the South Valley, with Canrobert to their left casting a long dark shadow over the grass. Then they were riding up the Causeway, with Epernon coming in fast from the flank and calling out softly, "All clear, they are well away to the northeast now."

They reined in their horses and spoke with him for a

while, their voices low. Bates looked over the battlefield below them for a long time and then turned to Jenny and said, "No one is moving. No one, not even a horse."

The floor of the valley was thick with the dead. Bates said urgently, "We'd better move to the west, Ma'am, I don't like it here."

She said firmly, "Where the dead are, Mr. Bates, that's where the wounded will be too."

"The bandsmen were here this afternoon. There'll be none left worth trying to save."

"The bandsmen were at the Alma too, where you found... Kirk."

"Aye, that's true enough. If it's only the boy we're looking for..."

She interrupted him, holding herself stiff and straight on the unaccustomed saddle. "For anyone I can help, Mr. Bates, you know that."

"Yes, Ma'am."

He turned his horse away and rode slowly to the left where Mahmoud was waiting, his horse prancing, smelling the blood down there. He said quietly, "Look for the boy, Mahmoud. For the horse Mandoh. Take your men to the right, I don't want the lady under the Russian guns if they are still nearby."

Mahmoud grinned. "They pull them back, Ingles, we don't have no trouble from the Russian guns, not anymore."

"All the same, take the right. We'll move down the valley to the left. Keep your men between us and the eastern end of the valley."

It was hard to think that the valley, where there had been so much of death, might now be free of the living who had caused the slaughter. It was as though the shadow of danger still hung over the hills long after the danger itself had gone and still made the valley, in the imaginings, a fearsome and frightening place, as though it might all come back without warning. It was as though they could not believe there could be so much blood and the instrument of that bleeding gone.

Mahmoud turned his horse and rode across their path, and Epernon came over and looked at him and understood, and stared down into the valley of death and said, "It is hard to believe that we can move among them now. I too feel it, there is a...how do you say it...a shroud hanging over all of us. I will ride beside you."

Slowly they rode down the Causeway into the valley.

The bright colors were all around them in the grass, the blues and scarlets of the uniforms, with their bright shining buttons and the broad bars of white that made such excellent targets across the soldiers' chests, the high cocked hats and plumes of the dead officers, and the shattered remains of their men. The flies were appalling, hanging in thick black clouds over the dead as the sun went down. And then, with the end of the last red rays of sunlight, the flies were suddenly gone too; the air was cold and damp and still.

Bates slipped off his horse and stood beside Jenny and said somberly, "Maybe you'd better wait, Miss Enderly, and leave it to us. If we find him..."

"No." Her mouth was a thin tight line. "No, I will search too. It won't be the first time that I've moved among the dead, looking for life."

"Aye, but this time..."

"This time too. This time, it's even more important than it was before. I'll not run away from it."

He nodded and held out his arms to help her down. There was one last word of warning, "I'll not have you move too far to the east, Ma'am. Don't move past the Bashi-Bazouk. I'll be close by you at all times, but when the dark comes there's going to be a bright moon, and it just might be that the Russians will pass this way again. They'll be probing again, searching out the weaknesses, and hoping to find them this time. For us, it's easy to ride off fast or to stand and fight and then run, but with you aboard..."

"I will not be in your way, Mr. Bates. Let's get to the work we have to do."

One of the Turks came over and took her horse. Silent, and dour, and unsmiling, he waited for her to move away, watching her, standing ready, as Mahmoud had told him, to get her mounted again in a hurry if the need should arise. With Bates beside her, and Epernon still mounted, sword drawn and riding close beside then, they began their hunt.

There were so many dead, it was impossible to count them.

Here, at the English end of the valley, the uniforms were all of the Lancers; the Dragoons, and the Hussars. They lay cold and still, staring up at the night sky with sightless eyes; some of them were very, very young.

Watching, Bates saw her turn a body over, then another and another and another. She said at last turning back to him, her voice low and controlled and steady, "This one is still alive, can you get him away for me?"

"Aye; Ma'am, I can do that."

He called out quietly for Mahmoud, and spoke to him, and Mahmoud called two of his men. And soon the young Dragoon, both legs shot away at the knees, was being carried gently away; there was no sound at all from his white lips.

They moved on. Bates waited while they passed through the lines of the Hussars, their cherry-colored trousers the same color now as their blood. It was the Lancers who lay around them now, the Seventeenth, and slowly, methodically Jenny was examining the bodies, touching them sometimes when this was all that was needed to see if there were any breath of life left. He wondered how she could bear the sight of so much carnage.

Soon it was dark, but the moon was bright and they moved on, stepping over the corpses, smelling the ripe scent of

THE CHARGE OF THE LIGHT BRIGADE

the blood.

It was Bates who found him first.

The mare, Mandoh, lay on her back, with her legs in, the air, one of them shattered by a shell. The ornately decorated saddle was lying to one side, its girth strap broken and wrenched away. Close by, Kirk lay on his face in the grass, and Bates crouched down beside him and put a hand on the still cold arm that lay at a strange angle, out-thrust and twisted round. When he tried to move it, he saw that it had been torn completely off at the shoulder. Gently, very carefully, he turned the boy over. The face was white and the eyes were open and staring, and he closed them before he looked up and called softly.

"Miss Enderly."

She came at once, knowing the truth before he could utter it. She stood there for a moment, looking down at the body; the right hand still held the sword, stiff and straight and angry. Soon, she dropped down to her knees and knelt there, and Bates turned away and waited. She sank slowly down onto her heels, staring down without any emotion at all on her thin face, and then she put a hand over the heart in what might have been, but was not, a mechanical gesture, a useless search for a heartbeat.

She held her hand there for a long time, as though deriving comfort from the touch, or perhaps trying still to impart it. She touched the cold face, and brushed a lank lock of hair away from the white forehead, and she stayed there for a long, long time.

In a little while, Bates walked away and spoke in whispers with Epernon, and whistled softly for Mahmoud and spoke with him too. And soon the men were all mounted again and waiting, standing there in the moonlight and the silence, their horses idly champing at the grass as their riders waited...

Bates went back to Jenny slowly. He crotched down on his heels besides her and said gently, "You must come away now, Miss Enderly."

She did not answer. He waited a while, and then said: "Is not good to wait too long. It's not good to think too much, not now." He waited, and then repeated urgently, "Come away now."

At last, she nodded. A frail and pathetic figure on the grass, her once-white dress gleaming in the moonlight, she looked at him with dark, somber eyes and said, "Can we bury him in the hills?"

"Aye, Ma'am, we can do that."

She sat there while be found a blanket and wrapped the body tightly in it, seeking to hide from her what she had already seen, seeking to make the broken body almost whole again, if not breathing with life. Then he stood up and cradled it in his strong arms and turned and moved away.

Jenny got to her feet and stumbled after him. Epernon looked at Mahmoud and gestured with his head, and the two of them moved out once more on the flanks, riding slowly as Bates and Jenny walked in silence between them. To one side of them, one of the Turks had a legless man slung carelessly over his shoulder.

Behind them the Bashi-Bazouk spread out in a wide arc, picking their way carefully over the fallen bodies, and soon, in silence, the little cortège was moving toward the hills that overlooked the plain and the two valleys, and the rivers beyond them.

Ahead, the mountains reared up high and severe and stark into the dark sky, a long steep climb in the cold of the night.

The bright moon hid behind the clouds; and all was darkness again.

The cortège was a broken shadow, moving in silence over the broken ground.

THE END

ABOUT THE AUTHOR

Alan Lyle-Smythe was born in Surrey, England. Prior to World War II, he served with the Palestine Police from 1936 to 1939 and learned the Arabic language. He was awarded an MBE in June 1938. He married Aliza Sverdova in 1939, then studied acting from 1939 to 1941.

In January 1940, Lyle-Smythe was commissioned in the Royal Army Service Corps. Due to his linguistic skills, he transferred to the Intelligence Corps and served in the Western Desert, in which he used the surname "Caillou" (the French word for 'pebble') as an alias.

He was captured in North Africa, imprisoned and threatened with execution in Italy, then escaped to join the British forces at Salerno. He was then posted to serve with the partisans in Yugoslavia. He wrote about his experiences in the book *The World is Six Feet Square* (1954). He was promoted to captain and awarded the Military Cross in 1944.

Following the war, he returned to the Palestine Police from 1946 to 1947, then served as a Police Commissioner in British-occupied Italian Somaliland from 1947 to 1952, where he was recommissioned a captain.

After work as a District Officer in Somalia and professional hunter, Lyle-Smythe travelled to Canada, where he worked as a hunter and then became an actor on Canadian television.

He wrote his first novel, *Rogue's Gambit*, in 1955, first using the name Caillou, one of his aliases from the war. Moving from Vancouver to Hollywood, he made an appearance as a contestant on the January 23 1958 edition of *You Bet Your Life*.

He appeared as an actor and/or worked as a screenwriter in such shows as *Daktari*, *The Man From U.N.C.L.E.* (including the screenwriting for "*The Bow-Wow Affair*" from 1965), *Thriller*, *Daniel Boone*, *Quark*, *Centennial*, and *How the West Was Won*. In 1966-67, he had a recurring role (as Jason Flood) in NBC's "*Tarzan*" TV series starring Ron Ely. Caillou appeared in such television movies as *Sole Survivor* (1970), *The Hound of the Baskervilles* (1972, as Inspector Lestrade), and *Goliath Awaits* (1981). His cinema film credits included roles in *Five Weeks in a Balloon* (1962), *Clarence, the Cross-Eyed Lion* (1965), *The Rare Breed* (1966), *The Devil's Brigade* (1968), *Hellfighters* (1968), *Everything You Always Wanted to Know About Sex* (*But Were Afraid to Ask)* (1972), *Herbie Goes to Monte Carlo* (1977), *Beyond Evil* (1980), *The Sword and the Sorcerer* (1982) and *The Ice Pirates* (1984).

Caillou wrote 52 paperback thrillers under his own name and the nom de plume of Alex Webb, with such heroes as Cabot Cain, Colonel Matthew Tobin, Mike Benasque, Ian Quayle and Josh Dekker, as well as writing many magazine stories.

Several of Caillou's novels were made into films, such as *Rampage* with Robert Mitchum in 1963, based on his big game hunting knowledge; *Assault on Agathon*, for which Caillou did the screenplay as well; and *The Cheetahs*, filmed in 1989.

He was married to Aliza Sverdova from 1939 until his death. Their daughter Nadia Caillou was the screenwriter for the film *Skeleton Coast*.

Alan Caillou died in Sedona, Arizona in 2006.

LOOKING FOR ACTION AND ADVENTURE
AUTHOR ALAN CAILLOU
NOVELS DELIVER!

AVAILABLE AT AMAZON.COM
FOR YOUR KINDLE OR IN PAPAERBACK

OR FROM
WWW.CALIBERCOMICS.COM

DON'T MISS ANY OF MICHAEL KASNER'S HARD HITTING MILITARY NOVEL SERIES

BLACK OPS

Formed by an elite cadre of government officials, the Black OPS team goes where the law can't - to seek retribution for acts of terror directed against Americans anywhere in the world.

3 BOOK SERIES

Armed with all the tactical advantages of modern technology, battle hard and ready when the free world is threatened - the Peacekeepers are the baddest grunts on the planet.

4 BOOK SERIES

CHOPPER COPS

America is being torn apart as criminal cartels terrorize our cities, dealing drugs and death wholesale. Local police are outgunned, so the President unleashes the U.S. TACTICAL POLICE FORCE. An elite army of super cops with ammo to burn, they swoop down on the hot spots in sleek high-tech attack choppers to win the dirty war and take back America!

4 BOOK SERIES

FROM CALIBER BOOKS
www.calibercomics.com

DON'T MISS ANY OF NEIL HUNTER'S NOVELS FROM CALIBER BOOKS

Reporter Les Mason is completing an expose on the Long Point Nuclear Plant. But before he can finish he dies an agonizing death. The doctors are baffled—and there are similar cases to follow...Chris Lane, his girlfriend, and organizer of the Long Point Protestors, discovers Mason's notes, and decides to find out for herself what the plant has to hide.

2 BOOK SERIES

In middle of the 21st century America – over-populated decaying cities are ruled by hi-tech gangs pushing every vice and wastelands are controlled by bands of mutants. Ordinary citizens are oppressed and face a hopeless future. But Marshal T.J. Cade is a new breed of law enforcer. Teamed with his cyborg partner, Janek, Cade takes on these criminals and works in the gray areas of the law to get the job done.

3 BOOK SERIES

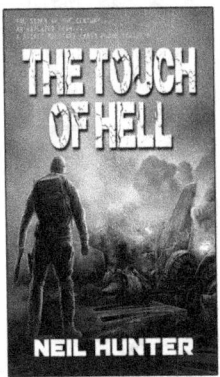

The village of Shepthorne England wasn't being gripped, but strangled by a winter's blanket of heavy snow and Arctic temperatures. The trouble began innocently enough with a massive pile-up of autos on frozen roads leading to and from the village. Then, from the sky, a military transport plane with its top secret cargo of devastation crashed down towards the center of the village. Hell was just beginning to touch Shepthorne and its unsuspecting citizens...

FROM CALIBER BOOKS
www.calibercomics.com

CALIBER COMICS GOES TO WAR!
HISTORICAL AND MILITARY THEMED GRAPHIC NOVELS

WORLD WAR ONE: NO MAN'S LAND

ISBN: 9781635298123

A look at World War 1 from the French trenches as they faced the Imperial German Army.

CORTEZ AND THE FALL OF THE AZTECS

ISBN: 9781635299779

Cortez battles the Aztecs while in search of Inca gold.

TROY: AN EMPIRE UNDER SIEGE

ISBN: 9781635298635

Homer's famous The Iliad and the Trojan War is given a unique human perspective rather than from the God's.

WITNESS TO WAR

ISBN: 9781635299700

WW2's Battle of the Bulge is seen up close by an embedded female war reporter.

THE LINCOLN BRIGADE

ISBN: 9781635298222

American volunteers head to Spain in the 1930s to fight in their civil war against the fascist regime.

EL CID: THE CONQUEROR

ISBN: 9780982654996

Europe's greatest warrior attempts to unify Spain against invading foreign and domestic armies.

WINTER WAR

ISBN: 9780985749392

At the outbreak of WW2 Finland fights against an invading Soviet army.

ZULUNATION: END OF EMPIRE

ISBN: 9780941613415

The global British Empire and far-reaching influence is threatened by a Zulu uprising in southern Africa.

AIR WARRIORS: WORLD WAR ONE #V1 - V4 *Take to the skies of WW1 as various fighter aces tell their harrowing stories.*
ISBN: 9781635297973 (V1), 9781635297980 (V2), 9781635297997 (V3), 9781635298000 (V4)

CALIBER COMICS PRESENTS
The Complete
VIETNAM JOURNAL

8 Volumes Covering the Entire Initial Run of the Critically Acclaimed Don Lomax Series

And Now Available
VIETNAM JOURNAL SERIES TWO
"INCURSION", "JOURNEY INTO HELL", "RIPCORD"

All new stories from Scott 'Journal' Neithammer as he reports durings the later stages of the Vietnam War.

CALIBER COMICS   WWW.CALIBERCOMICS.COM

FROM AWARD-WINNING COMIC WRITER AND ARTIST
WAYNE VANSANT
COMES TALES FROM WORLD WAR II

An action/adventure tale of the French Legionnaire soldier, Battron, who is involved with the liberation of a freebooting French ship, the Martel, from a heavily guarded Vichy French port during WWII. The Allies want the ship destroyed; the Germans have sent serious resources and firepower to save it. But a critical security leak in British intelligence could jeopardize not only the mission but Battron's life. The key is the beautiful former mistress of the Martel's captain, enlisted in the hope she can convince him to join the Free French movement with his ship. But has she told the Allies all she knows? And can Battron and his skillful commandos complete their dangerous mission in time under the luming shadow of the pending Allied invasion of North Africa?

Collection of tales involving the German Waffen SS from acclaimed creator and comic artist Wayne Vansant. These stories deal with the German Panzer troops during World War II and collects the highly acclaimed Battle Group Peiper story, Witches' Cauldon saga, along with three short tales. Knights of the Skull covers the war experiences of young German troops on the Eastern Front to the massacre of American troops near Malmedy Belgium to the harsh conditions of a crushing winter and engagements against an unrelenting Soviet troop onslaught.

The epic and incredible telling of the early days of the United States during the Second World War. Days of Darkness covers the darkest days of WWII for the US, when the country went from the tragedy of Pearl Harbor to the triumph at Midway. Covering in detail is the attack of the US Naval base and the devastation of the fleet in Hawaii, then the action moves to the evacuation and fall of the Philippines to the horror of the Death March of Bataan, and finally to the dramatic Battle of Midway which stopped the Japanese juggernaut in the Pacific.

"Heavy on authenticity, compellingly written and beautifully drawn." - Comics Buyers Guide.

WWW.CALIBERCOMICS.COM

ALSO AVAILABLE FROM CALIBER COMICS
QUALITY GRAPHIC NOVELS TO ENTERTAIN

THE SEARCHERS: VOLUME 1
The Shape of Things to Come

Before *League of Extraordinary Gentlemen* there was *The Searchers*. At the dawn of the 20th Century the greatest literary adventurers from the minds of Wells, Doyle, Burroughs, and Haggard were created. All thought to be the work of pure fiction. However, a century later, the real-life descendents of those famous characters are recuited by the legendary Professor Challenger in order to save mankind's future. Series collected for the first time.

"Searchers is the comic book I have on the wall with a sign reading - 'Love books? Never read a comic? Try this one! ....money back guarantee..." - Dark Star Books.

WAR OF THE WORLDS: INFESTATION

Based on the H.G. Wells classic! The "Martian Invasion" has begun again and now mankind must fight for its very humanity. It happened slowly at first but by the third year, it seemed that the war was almost over... the war was almost lost.

"Writer Randy Zimmerman has a fine grasp of drama, and spins the various strands of the story into a coherent whole... imaginative and very gritty."
- war-of-the-worlds.co.uk

HELSING: LEGACY BORN

From writer Gary Reed (Deadworld) and artists John Lowe (Captain America), Bruce McCorkindale (Godzilla). She was born into a legacy she wanted no part of and pushed into a battle recessed deep in the shadows of the night. Samantha Helsing is torn between two worlds...two allegiances...two families. The legacy of the Van Helsing family and their crusade against the "night creatures" comes to modern day with the most unlikely of all warriors.

"Congratulations on this masterpiece..."
- Paul Dale Roberts, Compuserve Reviews

DEADWORLD

Before there was The Walking Dead there was Deadworld. Here is an introduction of the long running classic horror series, Deadworld, to a new audience! Considered by many to be the godfather of the original zombie comic with over 100 issues and graphic novels in print and over 1,000,000 copies sold, Deadworld ripped into the undead with intelligent zombies on a mission and a group of poor teens riding in a school bus desperately try to stay one step ahead of the sadistic, Harley-riding King Zombie. Death, mayhem, and a touch of supernatural evil made Deadworld a classic and now here's your chance to get into the story!

DAYS OF WRATH

Award winning comic writer & artist Wayne Vansant brings his gripping World War II saga of war in the Pacific to Guadalcanal and the Battle of Bloody Ridge. This is the powerful story of the long, vicious battle for Guadalcanal that occurred in 1942-43. When the U.S. Navy orders its outnumbered and out-gunned ships to run from the Japanese fleet, they abandon American troops on a bloody, battered island in the South Pacific.

"Heavy on authenticity, compellingly written and beautifully drawn."
- Comics Buyers Guide

SHERLOCK HOLMES:
THE CASE OF THE MISSING MARTIAN

Sherlock is called out of retirement to London in 1908 to solve a most baffling mystery: The British Museum is missing a specimen of a Martian from the failed invasion of 1899. Did it walk away on its own or did someone steal it?

Holmes ponders the facts and remembers his part in the war effort alongside Professor Challenger during the War of the Worlds invasion that was chronicled in H.G. Wells' classic novel.

Meanwhile, Doctor Watson has problems of his own when his wife steals a scalpel from his surgical tool kit and returns to her old stomping grounds of Whitechapel, the London

CALIBER PRESENTS

The original Caliber Presents anthology title was one of Caliber's inaugural releases and featured predominantly new creators, many of which went onto successful careers in the comics' industry. In this new version, Caliber Presents has expanded to graphic novel size and while still featuring new creators it also includes many established professional creators with new visions. Creators featured in this first issue include nominees and winners of some of the industry's major awards including the Eisner, Harvey, Xeric, Ghastly, Shel Dorf, Comic Monsters, and more.

LEGENDLORE

From Caliber Comics now comes the entire Realm and Legendlore saga as a set of volumes that collects the long running critically acclaimed series. In the vein of The Lord of The Rings and The Hobbit with elements of Game of Thrones and Dungeon and Dragons.

Four normal modern day teenagers are plunged into a world they thought only existed in novels and film. They are whisked away to a magical land where dragons roam the skies, orcs and hobgoblins terrorize travelers, where unicorns prance through the forest, and kingdoms wage war for dominance. It is a world where man is just one race, joining other races such as elves, trolls, dwarves, changelings, and the dreaded night creatures who steal the night.

TIME GRUNTS

What if Hitler's last great Super Weapon was – Time itself! A WWII/time travel adventure that can best be described as *Band of Brothers* meets *Time Bandits*.

October, 1944. Nazi fortunes appear bleaker by the day. But in the bowels of the Wenceslas Mines, a terrible threat has emerged . . . The Nazis have discovered the ability to conquer time itself with the help of a new ominous device!

Now a rag tag group of American GIs must stop this threat to the past, present, and future . . . While dealing with their own past, prejudices, and fears in the process.

www.calibercomics.com

www.ingramcontent.com/pod-product-compliance
Lightning Source LLC
Chambersburg PA
CBHW072201070526
44585CB00015B/1238